PERSONALITY AND BODY LANGUAGE FOR THE HOSPITALITY PROFESSIONALS

Personality and Body Language for the Hospitality Professionals

NEERAJ AGARWAL

AMAN PUBLICATIONS
NEW DELHI

Published by
Rajiv Jain for Aman Publications
LG-4A, Ganpati Bhawan,
4675-B/21, Ansari Road,
Darya Ganj, Delhi-110002
E-mail: sshjbs@yahoo.com

2015

ISBN–81-8204-092-2
ISBN–978-81-8204-092-2

SOLE DISTRIBUTOR
JINDAL BOOK SERVICES
LG-4A, Ganpati Bhawan,
4675-B/21, Ansari Road,
Darya Ganj, Delhi - 110002

Jacket Designed by :
S.M. Graphics

Printed by:
Balaji Offest, Delhi, India

Preface

Body language is a kind of nonverbal communication, where thoughts, intentions, or feelings are expressed by physical behaviors, such as facial expressions, body posture, gestures, eye movement, touch and the use of space. Body language exists in both animals and humans, but this article focuses on interpretations of human body language. It is also known as kinesics.

People are constantly throwing off a storm of signals. These signals may be silent (non-verbal) messages communicated through the sender's body movements, facial expressions, voice tone and loudness.

Microexpressions, hand gestures, and posture register almost immediately, a silent orchestra that can have long-lasting repercussions.

Body language must not be confused with sign language, as sign languages are full languages like spoken languages and have their own complex grammar systems, as well as being able to exhibit the fundamental properties that exist in all languages. Body language, on the other hand, does not have a grammar and must be interpreted broadly, instead of having an absolute meaning corresponding with a certain movement, so it is not a language like sign language, and is simply termed as a "language" due to popular culture.

Personality means temperament, habits appearance, feelings, thoughts, behavior of a person. There are two main factors deciding the personality of a person. First is natural personality traits by birth second is an environmental effect. Natural temperament is also important but effects of environment are very crucial for developing a negative or positive personality.

If you want a successful career, you must develop a professional attitude and have a professional. With out proper attention on this area you canmot be a successful professional in today`s competitive world.

You always need good traits, god behavior, and good habits to enjoy a happy and successful life. A developed personality impressed everyone in Your home, Your office and Society.

Certainly you want to be a first type of person. Good personality is not a God gift everyone can achieve it. Most common areas of personality development are here: health, haire dress speech and body language.

This book is especially prepared for the hospitality professionals and the chapters which are related to body language and personality development are as follows: Body Language - An Element of Communication Skills, Understanding Body Language - Lesson for Hospitality Professionals, Body Language and Business Etiquette, Basics of Body Language, Facial Expressions, Importance of Body Language in Personality Development, Gesture, Stance, and Facial Expression, Customs and Etiquette, Hospitality Staff Taught to Read Body Language to Improve Customer Service Skills, 'Luxury Touch' Delivering in the Hospitality Industry, Body Language and Professionalism, Personality Development and Public Relations, Personality Traits, Importance of Personality Development, Soft Skills for Hospitality Industry, Communication and Listening Skills, Presentation Skills, Stress Management, Nonverbal Communication Training for Hospitality Industry, Skill Development - Concerns and Opportunities, Body Language of a Front Desk Officer, Managing Service Quality in Hospitality Industry Through Nonverbal Communication, Personality Development Tips for Hospitality Professionals.

Author

Contents

CHAPTER 1

Body Language - An Element of Communication Skills

INTRODUCTION

Body language is an important – and often decisive – factor in risk communication. This is especially true of communicators, who need to show congruency between the oral information and their body language when transmitting a message, because only if they manage to do so will the message be effective. Body language is an element in communication that we should be very much aware of because it gives clues to the character, emotions, and reactions of an individual.

Our state of mind is expressed in our body language. For example, if we doubt something we hear, we raise an eyebrow. If we feel puzzled, we scratch our nose. We cross our arms to isolate or protect ourselves. We shrug our shoulders to express indifference. We wink as a sign of intimacy. If we are impatient, we drum our fingers. We strike our forehead with our hand when we have forgotten something. We rock when we feel anxious, and we sway backwards and forwards on our feet when we are in a situation of conflict. An inexperienced speaker in an auditorium expresses his anxiety by moving from one side to another, staring at the ceiling, walking round in circles, or rubbing his hands together.

An awareness of body language is often the key to successful personal relationships and it can be the secret that enables so many people to manage others. Some individuals seem to have the knack of interpreting body language and manipulating people with their bodies as well as their voices. Knowledge of the body language of the other person and the ability to interpret it make a person aware of his or her own body language. This awareness, in turn, leads to greater self-control and more effective communication processes.

If you are aware of what you do with your body, your self-understanding becomes deeper and more meaningful. Once you manage to control your body language, you will be able to cross many defensive barriers and establish better relationships. Body language is an important component of communication and it is to our advantage to develop skills in this area in order to be better risk communicators. Presentation skill is a way in which an idea or scope needs to be discussed. A good presentation creates a good impression.

GENETIC AND CULTURAL ROOTS

It is difficult to determine exactly how a communication system is inherited or learned. Darwin believed that facial expressions of emotion were the same in all human beings, regardless of their culture.

Today it is considered that within a specific culture there exists a general agreement to recognize the different emotional states. The human brain is programmed to raise the corners of the mouth when the individual feels happy and turn them down when he is discontent. Depending on the sensation that reaches the brain, a person will frown, raise his eyebrows, or raise one side of his mouth.

The work of different researchers has shown that we can inherit in our genetic makeup certain basic physical reactions. We are born with elements of a body language. We can make another human being aware of basic sensations of hate, fear, pleasure, or sadness, without ever having learned how to do so. This does not contradict the fact that we do also have to learn many gestures that mean one thing in one society and something else in another.

The sound signals innate in the human being remain valid and continue to play important roles. Unlike verbal signals, they arise spontaneously and mean the same in all cultures. Shouting, sobbing, laughing, roaring, moaning, and crying transmit messages to everyone everywhere. Like the sounds of other species, these signals are associated with basic emotional states and give an immediate impression of the state of the person making the sounds.

The human being has conserved his instinctive expressions: the smile, laugh, stare, frightened face, and solemn face are signals proper to the species. These signals are common to all societies and persist despite the assimilation of many other cultural gestures.

The basic sounds and gestures of our species have their origin in the early stages of development of the human being. Crying is not only the first sign we give of our state of mind, but also the most fundamental one, shared with thousands of other species. There are certain expressions and standards that vary according to the culture, which are learned during the years of early childhood. These standards prescribe what should be done in response to the manifestation of each sensation or feeling in the different social environments. They vary according to social roles and demographic characteristics, and they differ from one culture to another.

POINTS TO REMEMBER

- Make Use visual slides as much as possible. Use of diagrams, charts is essential.
- Avoid too many clicks. It may confuse the user.
- Make use of facts and figures.

- Avoid the presentation to be very flashy or visually uncomfortable.
- Structure ideas of a presentation in a standardized way.
- Make sure the look and feel of the presentation is consistent.
- Try to know the audience with the help of presentation. It may reduce the discomfort.
- Avoid an abrupt end to the presentation.

WHY PRESENTATION SKILLS?

- Good presentation skills can drive the organization ahead by creating a positive impression
- It can express ideas more clearly without having them misunderstood.
- Use of colors and a professional look and feel catches the attention of the audience
- Use of visual aids helps in understanding concepts faster.

Body language plays an essential role in communicating with people. Body language comprises of the gestures and movements we make of the different parts of our body when communicating with people. Many a times, body language speaks more than words. Certainly, the body language must be in synch with the words.

POINTS TO REMEMBER

- Never be up tied or stiff while making movements.
- Avoid body language that may be misunderstood or look unprofessional. E.g. Winking
- A consistent eye contact is a positive sign and must be used
- Avoid fiddling with things around. It may distract the attention
- Each body part movement signifies something,and helps in interpreting, e.g. Standing with hands on hips signifies

aggressions, nodding signifies agreement and active listening, biting nails signifies nervousness.

- Unlike emails, body language does not give time to think. Hence they must be used appropriately.

WHY BODY LANGUAGE?

- Body language can instantly help to evaluate the interest of people
- It is a personal way of expressing emotions when words don't help
- It can communication interesting and non monotonous

POSITIVE BODY GESTURES

Positive body gestures are a sign of confidence and security. They are a sign of active participation and leave a good impression. Positive gestures include:

- Walking upright
- Shaking hands confidently
- Having a pleasant face.
- Nodding head is a positive gesture
- A steady eye contact

NEGATIVE BODY GESTURES

Following negative gestures are a sign of insecurity and restlessness. Such gestures show a lack of confidence. Such gestures should be avoided in interviews or meetings.

- Being up tied
- Biting nails
- Getting distracted

- Faking a smile
- Looking at something else while talking instead of the speaker
- Proper etiquettes should be followed.

LEADERSHIP SKILLS

Leadership skills are an important aspect from a professional and managerial perspective.

Leadership Skills Includes

- How well can you lead a team?
- How fast can you take decisions?
- How well can you encourage the team?

Points to remember

- A good leader must know how to communicate well
- Good Leadership skills means to ensure that the team believes and follows one goal.
- Every member needs to get equal attention. Partiality must be avoided
- Motivating the members to achieve the goal is important
- Leadership is not about dominating. Hence giving a chance to other members of leading at times is essential.
- Responsibilities should be fairly delegated.
- Practice what you preach! A good leader must possess all qualities he tries to inculcate in his team.
- Leadership skills involve evaluating risks, forecasting and taking instant decisions.

Why Leadership skills?

- Good leadership skills invite business opportunities
- Good leaders may make others feel important and needed. This increases productivity.
- They help to build relationships and rapport
- Good leaders can communicate effectively.
- Leaderships skills can solve problems instantly

Different types of leaderships

1. Autocratic Leader- He is more of a dictator who doesn't listen to anyone.

Advantage

- Has total authority
- Can make all decisions

Disadvantage

- May demotivate other employees.
- Other talented employees may not have a decision power.

2. Bureaucratic Leader: - Goes by the book to ensure no law or rule is broken

Advantage

- An organized way of leadership
- Used more in hospitals, banks and government offices to ensure security and go by law.

Disadvantage

- Has no scope of exploring new arenas
- There may be instances of frustration and anxiety to follow too many rules.

3. Transformational Leader: - this leader tries to inspire the team.

Advantage

- Motivates team
- Always looking for ideas to become efficient

Disadvantage

- May be misunderstood by others.
- The leader may sound commanding at times.

4. Laissez-faire Leader: - leaves most of the decisions on the employees

Advantage

- Allows other team members to speak and take decisions
- Needs little supervision

Disadvantage

- Results in lack of control and higher costs.
- Because of lack of supervision may lead to failures.

5. Democratic Leader: - Goes by the team. This leader is open to suggestions and decisions from other members.

Advantage

- Motivates team because the leader listens to the team.
- In case of difficulty the completing team acts like leaders and takes part in the decisions.

Disadvantage

- Not suited when quick decisions are required

- Since most of the team members are participating, it may lead to a chaos.

Planning is an essential aspect from both professional and personal perspective. It helps to look ahead and think of the future. A well documented plan is always essential to track status of present. A plan ideally defines the goals.

Points to Remember

- A plan should always be documented.
- It must always be to the point and consider the necessities of the business.
- It must offer a benchmark by which current status of the business can be reviewed.
- A well documented plan may not always guarantee success. However, a poorly documented plan can surely lead to a chaos.

Why Planning?

- It helps in taking faster decisions.
- It helps in forecasting and risk management
- Helps to avoid mistakes and dig hidden opportunities
- Helps to make thought process clearer.
- A plan should be periodically updated and reviewed marking the current scenarios.
- Planning is considered to be a stepping stone to success.

PLANNING - EXECUTION OF A PROJECT

The client gives his initial requirements. On complete analysis of his requirements, a project plan is made. In this plan, each requirement is broken into tasks to be allotted to the resources. Individual allotment of tasks is done for the employee depending on the work load. For each task, a planned start date and planned end date is noted. The planned hours for each task are also noted.

Once the plan is ready, it is sent to the client for approval. Once approved, the project implementation begins. As and when the tasks are undertaken, the plan is monitored and tracked. Tracking a plan would mean comparing the actual with the planned hours. This is to ensure that the deadlines are met.

Monitor a Plan

A plan needs to be continuously planned in order to meet the deadlines. This can be done by constantly keeping an eye on the tasks allotted to the resources. The actual work done must be noted and compared to the planned. Monitoring shows the actual deviation.

MOTIVATIONAL SKILLS

Motivation means encouragement. It's a driving force that helps any individual to move further. Many a times we are made to do the same job everyday. This is where motivation comes into picture. By motivating the individual he may be encouraged to work and bring new prospects and revenues.

Points to remember

- From a professional perspective motivation can be given in the form of perks, bonus etc.
- It may not always be monetary. Listening to grievances of the individual can be an important factor to motivate.
- Every individual has a different way of being motivated.
- Motivation skills are not just about how good can you motivate others; but how good can you motivate yourself.
- Creating challenges occasionally is also a form of motivation.

Why Motivations?

- Reduces boredom.

- Brings new prospects and revenues.
- Leads to job satisfaction and mental peace.
- Avoids jealousy and prejudice amongst team.
- Helps to achieve deadlines faster.

Ways of motivating

Students can be motivated by

- Giving a positive feedback on their assignments, projects etc
- Giving them new opportunities
- Creating a comfortable atmosphere in class
- Helping the students in the course
- Allowing them to participate in extra curricular activities
- Emphasizing on their hard work rather than grades

New and old employces can be motivated by

- Offering perks and incentives regularly
- Inceptives may not always be monetary
- For old employees, a friendly and supportive atmosphere matters
- To retain old employees, appraisals works the best
- Organizing events and programs to reduce monotony
- Sending employees on site.
- Giving them new challenges apart from their daily tasks.
- Appreciating their hard work.

SELF-CONFIDENCE

Self-confidence has a lot to do with ones own abilities. How well can one encourage himself to work and stand up for their rights. A self confident individual is confident and secured. He knows that he can achieve what he wants in spite of obstacles.

Points to remember

- Self-confidence can be enhanced by often rewarding your self.
- Prepare yourself for the worst.
- Be open to any task or activity.
- Focus on what you are doing without bothering about the obstacles.
- Body language conveys a lot about self-confidence.
- A positive attitude is the key to become self confident.
- If in a team; always speak up.
- Always be fearless.

Why Self-confidence?

- Self confident people have a positive approach keeping negative thoughts at bay.
- They help bringing prospects and meet deadlines
- Self confident people are mentally stable and can be an integral part of the team.
- Self confident people can encourage and motivate others.
- Self-confidence increases self esteem and respect for others.
- Helps to build relationships from a professional perspective.

How to develop Self-confidence?

- Self-confidence cannot be developed over night. Realizing your own faults and weaknesses is the first step to develop self-confidence

- Having a positive attitude
- Do things that you like the most. Indulge in activities that make you happy.
- Speak to people and be an active participant
- Keep yourself physically and mentally fit
- Pamper yourself and appreciate what others do for you
- Learn to prioritize things in your life.
- Not being conscience about small things and learn to move on.
- Accepting criticism and working towards the same.

DELEGATION SKILLS

Delegation means to authorize someone to work or complete your task. It must be noted that delegated tasks must be ethical. If a task is properly delegated, it can certainly save time and lead to success. Ideally only those tasks should be delegated in which you are good at. This is because delegation may require continuous support and supervision.

Points to remember

- A delegated task must always be approved and agreed upon.
- A poorly delegated task may lead to a failure and confusion
- Delegation must be properly used. A task must not be delegated by wish. There must be a valid reason for the same.
- Delegated tasks should be tracked continuously.
- They must be valid and possible.
- The person delegating the task must always be supportive and communicative.
- A good delegated task is always measurable, defined , achievable

- Always appreciate when the delegated job is complete.

Why Delegate?

- Saves time and motivates individuals
- It's a management technique to allow people explore new arenas.
- Helps to establish a rapport between high level and low level hierarchy.
- Helps to build trust.
- Leads to a better and higher efficiency.
- Allows better distribution of job.

When to Delegate?

- If the task to be delegated has sufficient information to be delegated.
- If the delegated task can be monitored.
- If the delegated task can provide some skills to the individual
- If the deadlines are stringent.
- If the person whom the task is being delegated does not have a work load.

How to Delegate?

- Identify the task properly.
- Identify the risks involved, constraints etc.
- One needs to be patient. You may be an expert in the domain. The individual may not be.
- Try and involve more people in the delegation
- The delegated task must be always agreed upon and not forced.

- The task must be monitored.

Whom to Delegate?

- The person's skill and experience must be considered.
- How comfortable is the person in accepting the delegated task?
- The person should not be overloaded with other priority work.

TIME MANAGEMENT

Time management is the most commonly talked about topic in almost every field. Individuals have too many high priority tasks. However the only issue is that how well can they manage the time or distribute the time to finish them. This problem is faced by almost everyone, be it the CEO of a company or an employee. The most important factor of time management is as to how effectively be the time utilized.

Points to Remember

- Always high priority tasks must be completed first.
- Ambience of the place matters a lot.
- Each task must be reasonably allotted the time.
- The key to an effective time management is to know your goals properly.
- Time management skills don't come overnight. It is developed with practice.
- Delegating a task leads to a better time management.
- The managed tasks must be monitored to ensure they aren't exceeding the time frame.
- Make use of available resources. You may be spending time on getting some information already available or known to someone else.

Why Manage Time?

- Increases efficiency
- Reduces anxiety and work pressure.
- Motivates people and introduces confidence
- Leads to a better estimation of tasks.

Time management is to ensure that the end product is delivered in time and has quality, productive and efficient.

How to Manage Time?

- Make the plan well in advance.
- Prioritize the important tasks.
- Have an awareness of the tasks.
- Create a schedule of managing time that is flexible. This is important to ensure that changes in time can be accommodated
- Make decisions instantly
- Monitor the time management schedule.
- The schedule should not be on a very broad perspective. Its must consider managing time on a daily basis.
- Activity logs are the most common way to manage time. These logs give details of all activities performed.
- Always keep alternatives ready.
- Work as a team and support colleagues

ATTITUDES

Good attitudes contribute to success.

Introduction

Acquiring good attitudes can alter lives. Good attitudes contribute to success. An executive can't excel without good attitude. It is a critical factor in success. A person always proved to be team player with good attitude.

There are various factors that influence one's attitude such as school, work, media, cultural background, traditions and beliefs. For example, in a country with an honest government, you will always find people with right attitude - honest, trustworthy and helpful.

- People with good attitudes have following features:
- They are pleasing character since they believe in themselves.
- They are naturally very energetic.
- They enjoy life with full extent.
- They never take back seat motivating other.
- They are always good team player.

Bad attitudes attribute ill health, high stress, low productivity, purposeless life, fewer friends etc.

You can acquire positive attitude by becoming aware of the traits that build positive attitudes. Like the way you feed body with good food, you should also feed your mind with good thoughts.

Attitude can be considered as an individual's outlook towards something. Something could be another person, behavior or some event. Certainly an attitude should always be positive. It keeps negative thinking at bay and gets a feeling of confidence. A positive attitude should not be to an extent that it hurts sentiments of masses.

Points to Remember

- The key to a positive attitude is to accept failures.
- One should not give up very easily and strive for success.
- Looking for alternatives (solutions).
- Believing in yourself and always be open to criticism
- Having a negative attitude can be stressful, affect self esteem
- Attitude has got nothing to do with arrogance. It is mere a perspective.

- Being "fake" is a sign of not being yourself. This will not work for having a positive attitude.

Why Attitude?

- Positive attitude keeps a person healthier both physically and mentally.
- Helps achieve goals and success.
- Gives a sense of superiority and happiness
- A positive attitude helps to deal with stress.
- A positive attitude at work can help achieve goals faster.

Types of Attitude

- **Positive attitude**: - People who always think positively have a positive attitude. People with a positive attitude are usually confident, respect others and are always in search of new arenas. A positive attitude at work is very essential.
- **Negative attitude**: - People who think negatively have a negative attitude. Categories of people who flaunt for no reason also fall in this category. People who always underestimate others and have a superiority complex can also have a negative attitude.

Approach to a Positive Attitude

- Be aware of the surroundings
- Accept the way you are
- Do things that relax you more frequently
- Always think positive
- Seeking opportunities always
- Looking for alternative solutions
- Believing in yourself

Reason of developing negative attitude

- Negative thinking
- Worrying about small issues
- At times, people have a negative attitude by will.
- Loosing faith in your self.

Commonsense

Commonsense - Sixth sense.

We have five senses naturally gifted. Applying these senses, we can acquire sixth sense, i.e. commonsense. You can be highly educated, but if you lacks commonsense, you won't be able to excel high in career or business. Commonsense can't be taught, you have to acquire it with constant effort. An education without commonsense is worthless.

Commonsense means a very natural, comprehensive or radical thinking. It is an approach to take decisions as fast as possible in tight situations. It means that we must pay attention to something that is likely to happen or obvious.

Points to remember

- Common sense is not an "art "or "practice" that comes by experience.
- Common sense differs from person to person
- Common sense has got nothing to do with intelligence.
- How well can a person use his knowledge is also a part of common sense.

Why Commonsense?

- Helps to take faster decisions to avoid chaos
- Helps to achieve confidence and success
- Helps to become alert

- A person with commonsense is supposed to be reasonable
- Helps to develop skills.

Common sense reasoning

Our ability to use common sense depends on how well can we reason common sense. This includes:

- Ability to reason quickly
- Spontaneity
- Ability to tolerate inconsistency and faults
- Ability to handle situations that change with respect to events
- Ability to pay attention to the obvious

SELF ESTEEM

Self-esteem is very important in order to enjoy in whatever you are doing. It gives good feeling and drives you to achieve more and more. Lack of it means lack of self-respect. In that case, ego takes the driver's seat and leads to rust you. You will find yourself prompt in giving excuses, you will become lazy and enjoy being idle.

There is correlation between feelings and behavior. If feeling are good, you behavior will bound to be good. Self-esteem gives you good feeling, enthusiasm and energy.

There are two kinds of people, givers and takers. Givers sleep well and always have high self-esteem while takers eat well and lack self-esteem.

Low-esteemed people lacks vision, thus can't acquire excellence.

Self esteem is a way by which a person can realize his own worth. Worth and emotions include confidence, alertness, pride etc. it is a feeling that is developed by itself and grows naturally. Self esteem is how well you can accept yourself.

Points to Remember

- Self esteem may differ from person to person.
- Self esteem can be increased by:-
- Pampering your self.
- Not feeling guilty or conscience
- Not being judgmental about others.
- Accepting yourself the way you are and changing for good.
- Always being optimistic and being prepared for the worst

Why Self-esteem?

- Increases confidence
- Gives a proud feeling thereby increasing productivity
- Helps managing work and being not being partial.
- Strengths can be determined.
- Makes an individual feel important and increased self worth.

CHAPTER 2

Understanding Body Language - Lesson for Hospitality Professionals

"The problem with communication ... is the illusion that it has been accomplished."

—***George Bernard Shaw***

Like many other industries, the everyday environment of hospitality includes some very useful high tech tools that help project revenues, identify the level of sales booking pace, manage inventory, monitor payroll and more.

It remains essential though in our world of welcoming people to our establishments that we retain a solid focus on the "high touch" side of the every-day interactions with people.

Understanding body language is a talent that can increase your successes in life. You can recognize what a person feels and likely thinks by examining their subliminal body language. This can be both a business and social skill that allows you to better communicate and interact with the people in your life over the long haul.

A person's words may be hinting one message to you, but her/ his body language could be sending a conflicting signal. Through body movements, lack of or full eye contact, facial expressions and gestures, you can often read into a person's genuine intentions. As a rule, body language communicates more about what someone says than what her/his own words do.

People in the business community use body language interpretation everyday when they interview potential employees. When they interpret body language, they are looking for a variety of movements that indicate if the person is uncomfortable answering certain questions or talking about particular subjects.

If you observe that s/he is uncomfortable about certain points on their resume, their body language may provide you a better analysis of past employment experience than the words and resume combined. Body language is often used in the legal system as well, as noted that when a witness is testifying, their attorney will frequently advise them to make proper eye contact with certain other parties (such as the jury) in the courtroom in an effort to build credibility.

LESSONS FOR HOSPITALITY PROFESSIONALS

The reason is not hard to grasp – we hear the spoken word, but it is our body language or verbal communication that tell us almost instantly if we have made a connection.

For example, if we send a direct mail piece about our hotel in Kentucky to a reader that has never been to the Blue Grass state, they will likely pitch the flyer, as they have no connection. If they take a phone call from someone they know slightly about the Lexington area, they might have a possible interest in the University, but they may not like doing business by phone.

On the other hand, if we get a face-to-face meeting and "see" by the person's responses what motivates the person about the city – the ball team, the library, the gardens, architecture, the business department, the caliber of graduates from a certain program or whatever, then the connection is made.

There are entire books written about body language, and the internet has thousands of articles, advertisements and ideas. I ask readers to consider the following as starting points:

- Avoid putting obstructions between you and the other person, such as a briefcase, a package or presentation piece. This is applicable when speaking with staff or potential clients.
- Do not sit behind a desk, but keep the communication flow smooth.
- Learn about people's private space, which varies by gender, age and race. The closer they are, generally the warmer their opinions are of you. The farther away that someone is, the less they care. It is worth noting that personal space is culturally sensitive; what is considered close in one country is far away in another.
- Do not make others feel uncomfortable. This can be handled by ensuring the words spoken are comprehended by the other party – their body language will tell you if they understand.
- The eyes are a primary key to understanding. People who look away while supposedly listening to you are often thinking about something else. This is why when you are talking to a group of people, if an item in conversation interests someone who may be looking away, they will ask for you to repeat the story. Some cultures believe that looking at someone in the eyes is a sign of disrespect, so we must be sensitive to the cultural diversity in our hospitality businesses.
- Use your hands to demonstrate your point if that is your style, but do not point AT the other person.
- Watch for people's habits, as some may be nervous, but others can be using negotiating and stall tactics.
- Recognize what agreement signs are, such as subtle nodding, slight smiles and the inclination to complete the business being discussed.
- Recognize what disagreement signs are such as wandering eyes, frowns or folded arms.
- Learn to read signs of closure or acceptance, such as crossed legs or leaning inwards.

ESSENTIALS OF BODY LANGUAGE IN HOSPITALITY SECTOR

Body language is the non-verbal movements we make as a part of how we communicate, from waving hands to involuntary twitching of facial muscles.

- Uses of non-verbal communication: How non-verbal communication is used.
- Reading non-verbals: Basics of non-verbal communication.
- Mehrabian's communication study: 7% words, 38% tone, 55% body language?
- Haptic communication: Communicating by touch.
- Kinesic communication: Communicating by body movement.
- Proxemic communication: Communicating by body positioning.
- Gesture types: Emblems and more.
- Tells: Unconscious signals.

Don'ts

1. **Don't cross your arms or legs** – You have probably already heard you shouldn't cross your arms as it might make you seem defensive or guarded. This goes for your legs too. Keep your arms and legs open.
2. **Have eye contact, but don't stare** – If there are several people you are talking to, give them all some eye contact to create a better connection and see if they are listening. Keeping too much eye-contact might creep people out. Giving no eye-contact might make you seem insecure. If you are not used to keeping eye-contact it might feel a little hard or scary in the beginning but keep working on it and you'll get used to it.
3. **Don't be afraid to take up some space** – Taking up space by for example sitting or standing with your legs apart a bit

signals self-confidence and that you are comfortable in your own skin.

4. **Relax your shoulders** – When you feel tense it's easily winds up as tension in your shoulders. They might move up and forward a bit. Try to relax. Try to loosen up by shaking the shoulders a bit and move them back slightly.
5. **Nod when they are talking** – nod once in a while to signal that you are listening. But don't overdo it and peck like Woody Woodpecker.
6. **Don't slouch, sit up straight** – but in a relaxed way, not in a too tense manner.
7. **Lean, but not too much** – If you want to show that you are interested in what someone is saying, lean toward the person talking. If you want to show that you're confident in yourself and relaxed lean back a bit. But don't lean in too much or you might seem needy and desperate for some approval. Or lean back too much or you might seem arrogant and distant.
8. **Smile and laugh** – lighten up, don't take yourself too seriously. Relax a bit, smile and laugh when someone says something funny. People will be a lot more inclined to listen to you if you seem to be a positive person. But don't be the first to laugh at your own jokes, it makes you seem nervous and needy. Smile when you are introduced to someone but don't keep a smile plastered on your face, you'll seem insincere.
9. **Don't touch your face** – it might make you seem nervous and can be distracting for the listeners or the people in the conversation.
10. **Keep you head up** - Don't keep your eyes on the ground, it might make you seem insecure and a bit lost. Keep your head up straight and your eyes towards the horizon.
11. **Slow down a bit** – this goes for many things. Walking slower not only makes you seem more calm and confident, it will also

make you feel less stressed. If someone addresses you, don't snap you're neck in their direction, turn it a bit more slowly instead.

12. **Don't fidget** – try to avoid, phase out or transform fidgety movement and nervous ticks such as shaking your leg or tapping your fingers against the table rapidly. You'll seem nervous and fidgeting can be a distracting when you try to get something across. Declutter your movements if you are all over the place. Try to relax, slow down and focus your movements.

13. **Use your hands more confidently** – instead of fidgeting with your hands and scratching your face use them to communicate what you are trying to say. Use your hands to describe something or to add weight to a point you are trying to make. But don't use them to much or it might become distracting. And don't let your hands flail around, use them with some control.

14. **Lower your drink** – don't hold your drink in front of your chest. In fact, don't hold anything in front of your heart as it will make you seem guarded and distant. Lower it and hold it beside your leg instead.

15. **Realise where you spine ends** – many people (including me until recently) might sit or stand with a straight back in a good posture. However, they might think that the spine ends where the neck begins and therefore crane the neck forward in a Montgomery Burns-pose. Your spine ends in the back of your head. Keep you whole spine straight and aligned for better posture.

16. **Don't stand too close** – one of the things we learned from Seinfeld is that everybody gets weirded out by a close-talker. Let people have their personal space, don't invade it.

17. **Mirror** - Often when you get along with a person, when the two of you get a good connection, you will start to mirror each other unconsciously. That means that you mirror the other

person's body language a bit. To make the connection better you can try a bit of proactive mirroring. If he leans forward, you might lean forward. If she holds her hands on her thighs, you might do the same. But don't react instantly and don't mirror every change in body language. Then weirdness will ensue

18. Keep a good attitude – last but not least, keep a positive, open and relaxed attitude. How you feel will come through in your body language and can make a major difference.

PERFECT YOUR BODY LANGUAGE

It's not what you say but how you say it. And sometimes, it's how you're perceived. Covert, unconscious responses to body language cues still reflect discrimination against women, especially those taking on a leadership role. Since hiring, salary and promotion (especially to top positions) often depend on being recognized as an emergent leader, this puts females at a distinct disadvantage.

Employees look for and emulate the nonverbal signals they get from their bosses. Current leaders can help create a level playing field for emergent leaders by providing the same positive cues when listening to women as they do when listening to men.

So, to groom women for top positions, offer females the coaching, mentors and career opportunities that develop leadership potential. And, women, pay attention to these five body language cues:

Eye Contact

It is so powerful because it is instinctive and connected with humans' early survival patterns. Children who could attract and maintain eye contact, and therefore increase attention, had the best chance of being fed and cared for. As adults, we still put a lot of credence in the signals we give and get from each other's eyes.

As long as someone is looking at us, we believe we have their interest. A sure sign that a conversation is lagging is when one of

Managing Effective Communication

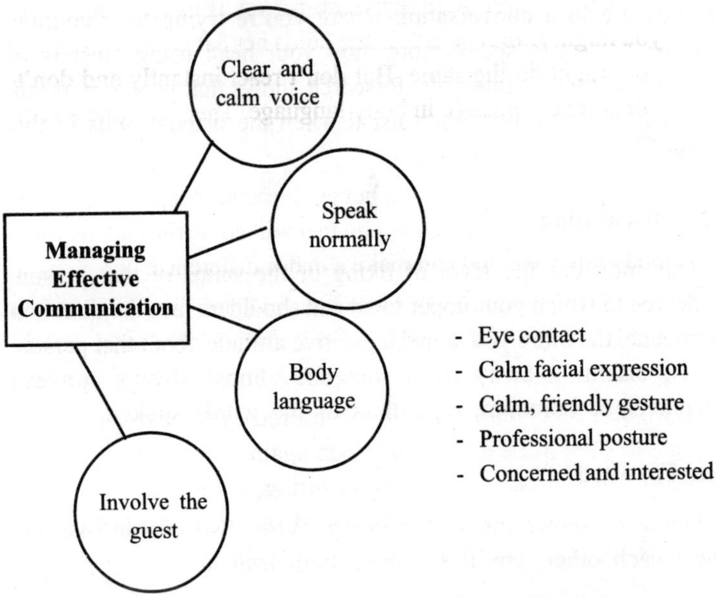

the participants begins looking away to pay more attention to other people or objects in the vicinity. And when she glances at her watch, gazes blankly into the distance or visually scans the room, she is giving definite signals with her eyes that she has, in effect, stopped listening.

Smiles

Smiles have a powerful effect on all of us. The human brain prefers happy faces, recognizing them more quickly than those with negative expressions. Employees instinctively pay more attention to the facial expressions of those around them. People search for smiles or frowns to get a better sense of how to interpret and react to a situation, and then they begin to mimic the predominant emotions.

Head Nods

These are recognized in most cultures as indicators of approval, understanding or agreement. When someone nods slowly, it usually indicates an ongoing interest in whomever is speaking. The next time you are in a conversation where you're trying to encourage the other person to speak more, nod your head using clusters of three nods at regular intervals. Research shows that people will talk three to four times more than usual when the listener nods in this fashion.

Body Orientation

This indicates the level of liking or the status of that person. The degree to which your upper torso and shoulders face the direction of someone, the more you signal a positive attitude about that person. In fact, orienting away from someone almost always conveys detachment or boredom, regardless of the words spoken.

Lean Forward

Doing so shows interest or liking. When two people like and respect each other, you'll see them both lean in.

A HAPPY GUEST . . . .

- Returns the next time.
- Reocmmends the place to his friends and acquaintances.
- Avails other services of hotel.
- Appreciates the hotel staff and respects them.
- And thus, the profits are increased

CHAPTER 3

Body Language and Business Etiquette

Body language can make or break a deal. How you carry yourself when engaged in conversation is often as important as what you say. Body language is nonverbal, but it communicates volumes about you nonetheless.

With almost infinite symbolic interpretations for body language, no wonder people are nervous about it! Your best bet is to know about some of the body-language pits you can fall into and how to avoid them.

STANDING

When you stand, keep your back straight, middle section in alignment with your back, shoulders back, and head up. This posture connotes comfort with yourself and ease in the situation. Slouching, sticking your belly out, stuffing your hands in your pockets, and folding your arms defensively all suggest aggressive unease.

SITTING

Take care in the way you sit, for no other position connotes so much on its own. Think of the diversity of sitting positions that you've seen in business meetings, from practically horizontal to alert and upright. Sit with a straight back and with your legs together in front of you or crossed, either at the knee or at the ankle. Normally, women don't cross their legs, but men are allowed. Avoid jiggling your knee, which is a sign of nervousness (and can be pretty annoying to people sitting near you).

HANDS

Some people talk with their hands; others stand with their hands glued to their sides. Most people haven't the foggiest notion what their hands are doing when they talk.

Using your hands can be effective sometimes, aggressive sometimes, and irrelevant most of the time. Controlling your hands takes effort and willpower. Monitor your hand movements. Avoid making sweeping, cappuccino-clearing gestures during meetings. If you have to, sit on your hands.

HEAD MOVEMENTS

Head movements communicate important information. Nodding in agreement can be immensely helpful to others, but too much nodding makes you look like a bobble-head doll. Shaking your head can signal disagreement or disapproval, but avoid shaking your head too much.

FACIAL EXPRESSIONS

Facial expressions are crucial in your repertoire of body language. No other part of your body can convey the immense richness of nonverbal communication that your face does. For example:

- Smiles are important signals of generosity and nonaggression. But forced smiles signal that you can barely tolerate the other person.
- Likewise, frowns signal disagreement, disapproval, and sometimes anger. But they can also suggest hard thinking and focused concentration.

These facial expressions are the most obvious ones, but hundreds of others exist: an arched eyebrow, flared nostrils, a bitten lip, a grimace . . . and on and on. Every one of them has a culturally agreed-on set of meanings.

Take a day to monitor your most frequently used facial expressions and assess their appropriateness and their effectiveness. You'll probably be surprised by the types of messages your expressions transmit!

EYES

Maintain eye contact when talking with others. Do not study your hands or clean your fingernails while others are talking. When talking in a group, make eye contact with everyone; don't focus on only one person.

CHAPTER 4

Basics of Body Language

Body language is a powerful concept which successful people tend to understand well.

The study and theory of body language has become popular in recent years because psychologists have been able to understand what we 'say' through our bodily gestures and facial expressions, so as to translate our body language, revealing its underlying feelings and attitudes.

Body Language is also referred to as 'non-verbal communications', and less commonly 'non-vocal communications'.

The term 'non-verbal communications' tends to be used in a wider sense, and all these terms are somewhat vague.

For the purposes of this article, the terms 'body language' and 'non-verbal communications' are broadly interchangeable. This guide also takes the view that body language/non-verbal communications is the study of how people communicate face-to-face aside from the spoken words themselves, and in this respect the treatment of the subject here is broader than typical body language guides limited merely to body positions and gestures.

If you carry out any serious analysis or discussion you should clarify the terminology in your own way to suit your purposes.

For example:

- Does body language include facial expression and eye movement? - Usually, yes.
- What about breathing and perspiration? - This depends on your definition of body language.
- And while tone and pitch of voice are part of verbal signals, are these part of body language too? - Not normally, but arguably so, especially as you could ignore them if considering only the spoken words and physical gestures/ expressions.
- There are no absolute right/wrong answers to these questions. It's a matter of interpretation.
- A good reason for broadening the scope of body language is to avoid missing important signals which might not be considered within a narrow definition of body language.
- Nevertheless confusion easily arises if definitions and context are not properly established, for example:

It is commonly and carelessly quoted that 'non-verbal communications' and/or 'body language' account for up to 93% of the meaning that people take from any human communication. This statistic is actually a distortion based on Albert Mehrabian's research theory, which while itself is something of a cornerstone of body language research, certainly did not make such a sweeping claim.

Mehrabian's research findings in fact focused on communications with a strong emotional or 'feelings' element. Moreover the 93% non-verbal proportion included vocal intonation (paralinguistics), which are regarded by many as falling outside of the body language definition.

Care must therefore be exercised when stating specific figures relating to percentages of meaning conveyed, or in making any firm claims in relation to body language and non-verbal communications.

It is safe to say that body language represents a very significant proportion of meaning that is conveyed and interpreted between people. Many body language experts and sources seem to agree that that between 50-80% of all human communications are non-verbal. So while body language statistics vary according to situation, it is generally accepted that non-verbal communications are very important in how we understand each other (or fail to), especially in face-to-face and one-to-one communications, and most definitely when the communications involve an emotional or attitudinal element.

Body language is especially crucial when we meet someone for the first time.

We form our opinions of someone we meet for the first time in just a few seconds, and this initial instinctual assessment is based far more on what we see and feel about the other person than on the words they speak. On many occasions we form a strong view about a new person before they speak a single word.

Consequently body language is very influential in forming impressions on first meeting someone.

The effect happens both ways - to and from:

- When we meet someone for the first time, their body language, on conscious and unconscious levels, largely determines our initial impression of them.
- In turn when someone meets us for the first time, they form their initial impression of us largely from our body language and non-verbal signals.

And this two-way effect of body language continues throughout communications and relationships between people.

Body language is constantly being exchanged and interpreted between people, even though much of the time this is happening on an unconscious level.

Remember - while you are interpreting (consciously or unconsciously) the body language of other people, so other people are constantly interpreting yours.

The people with the most conscious awareness of, and capabilities to read, body language tend to have an advantage over those whose appreciation is limited largely to the unconscious.

You will shift your own awareness of body language from the unconscious into the conscious by learning about the subject, and then by practising your reading of non-verbal communications in your dealings with others.

BODY LANGUAGE IS MORE THAN BODY POSITIONS AND MOVEMENTS

Body language is not just about how we hold and move our bodies.

Body language potentially (although not always, depending on the definition you choose to apply) encompasses:

- how we position our bodies
- our closeness to and the space between us and other people (proxemics), and how this changes
- our facial expressions
- our eyes especially and how our eyes move and focus, etc
- how we touch ourselves and others
- how our bodies connect with other non-bodily things, for instance, pens, cigarettes, spectacles and clothing
- our breathing, and other less noticeable physical effects, for example our heartbeat and perspiration

Body language tends not to include:

- the pace, pitch, and intonation, volume, variation, pauses, etc., of our voice.

Arguably this last point should be encompassed by body language, because a lot happens here which can easily be missed if we consider merely the spoken word and the traditional narrow definition of body language or non-verbal communications.

Voice type and other audible signals are typically not included in body language because they are audible 'verbal' signals rather than physical visual ones, nevertheless the way the voice is used is a very significant (usually unconscious) aspect of communication, aside from the bare words themselves.

Consequently, voice type is always important to consider alongside the usual body language factors.

Similarly breathing and heartbeat, etc., are typically excluded from many general descriptions of body language, but are certainly part of the range of non-verbal bodily actions and signals which contribute to body language in its fullest sense.

More obviously, our eyes are a vital aspect of our body language.

Our reactions to other people's eyes - movement, focus, expression, etc - and their reactions to our eyes - contribute greatly to mutual assessment and understanding, consciously and unconsciously.

With no words at all, massive feeling can be conveyed in a single glance. The metaphor which describes the eyes of two lovers meeting across a crowded room is not only found in old romantic movies. It's based on scientific fact - the strong powers of non-verbal communications.

These effects - and similar powerful examples - have existed in real human experience and behaviour for thousands of years.

The human body and our instinctive reactions have evolved to an amazingly clever degree, which many of us ignore or take for granted, and which we can all learn how to recognize more clearly if we try.

Our interpretation of body language, notably eyes and facial expressions, is instinctive, and with a little thought and knowledge we can significantly increase our conscious awareness of these signals: both the signals we transmit, and the signals in others that we observe.

Doing so gives us a significant advantage in life - professionally and personally - in our dealings with others.

Body language is not just reading the signals in other people.

Importantly, understanding body language enables better self-awareness and self-control too.

We understand more about other people's feelings and meanings, and we also understand more about these things in ourselves.

When we understand body language we become better able to refine and improve what our body says about us, which generates a positive improvement in the way we feel, the way we perform, and what we achieve.

Body Language Definitions

As explained, the terms body language and non-verbal communications are rather vague.

So what is body language? And more usefully, what might we regard it to be, if we are to make the most of studying and using it?

The *Oxford English Dictionary* (revised 2005) definition is:

> "**body language** - noun - the conscious and unconscious movements and postures by which attitudes and feelings are communicated [for example]: his intent was clearly expressed in his body language."

The *Oxford Business English Dictionary* offers a slightly different definition. Appropriately and interestingly the *Oxford Business English Dictionary* emphasizes the sense that body language can be used as a tool, rather than it being an involuntary effect with no particular purpose:

> "**body language** - noun - the process of communicating what you are feeling or thinking by the way you place and move your body rather than by words [for example]: The course trains sales people in reading the customer's body language."

The *OED dictionary* definition of **kinesics** - the technical term for the study of body language (and more loosely of body language itself) - depends on the interpretation of 'non-verbal communication':

> "**kinesics** - the study of the way in which certain body movements and gestures serve as a form of non-verbal communication... [and] body movements and gestures regarded as a form of non-verbal communication."

Body language is more than those brief descriptions.

- Body language certainly also encompasses where the body is in relation to other bodies (often referred to as 'personal space').
- Body language certainly also includes very small bodily movements such as facial expressions and eye movements.
- Body language also arguably covers all that we communicate through our bodies apart from the spoken words (thereby encompassing breathing, perspiration, pulse, blood-pressure, blushing, etc.)

In this respect, standard dictionary definitions don't always describe body language fully and properly.

We could define body language more fully as:

- "Body language is the unconscious and conscious transmission and interpretation of feelings, attitudes, and moods, through:
- body posture, movement, physical state, position and relationship to other bodies, objects and surroundings,
- facial expression and eye movement, (and this transmission and interpretation can be quite different to the spoken words)."

Words alone - especially emotional words (or words used in emotional situations) - rarely reflect full or true meaning and motive.

We find clues to additional or true meaning in body language.

Being able to 'read' body language therefore helps us greatly:

- to know how people feel and what they mean, and
- to understand better how people might be perceiving our own non-verbal signals, and (often overlooked)
- to understand ourselves better, deeper than the words we hear ourselves saying.

BODY LANGUAGE - BACKGROUND AND HISTORY

Philosophers and scientists have connected human physical behaviour with meaning, mood and personality for thousands of years, but only in living memory has the study of body language become as sophisticated and detailed as it is today.

Body language studies and written works on the subject are very sparse until the mid-1900s.

The first known experts to consider aspects of body language were probably the ancient Greeks, notably Hippocrates and Aristotle, through their interest in human personality and behaviour, and the Romans, notably Cicero, relating gestures to feelings and communications. Much of this early interest was in refining ideas about oration - speech-making - given its significance to leadership and government.

Isolated studies of body language appeared in more recent times, for example Francis Bacon in Advancement of Learning, 1605, explored gestures as reflection or extension of spoken communications. John Bulwer's Natural History of the Hand published in 1644, considered hand gestures. Gilbert Austin's Chironomia in 1806 looked at using gestures to improve speech-making.

Charles Darwin in the late 1800s could be regarded as the earliest expert to have made serious scientific observation about body language, but there seems little substantial development of ideas for at least the next 150 years.

Darwin's work pioneered much ethological thinking. Ethology began as the science of animal behaviour. It became properly established during the early 1900s and increasingly extends to human behaviour and social organization. Where ethology considers animal evolution and communications, it relates strongly to human body language. Ethologists have progressively applied their findings to human behaviour, including body language, reflecting the evolutionary origins of much human non-verbal communication - and society's growing acceptance of evolutionary rather than creationist theory. Austrian zoologist and 1973 Nobel Prizewinner Konrad Lorenz (1903-89) was a founding figure in ethology. Desmond Morris, author of The Naked Ape, discussed below, is an ethologist, as is the evolutionary biologist Richard Dawkins (b. 1941) a leading modern thinker in the field. Ethology, like psychology, is an over-arching science which continues to clarify the understanding of body language.

The popular and accessible study of body language as we know it today is very recent.

In his popular 1971 book 'Body Language', Julius Fast (1919-2008) wrote:

> "...kinesics [body language and its study] is still so new as a science that its authorities can be counted on the fingers of one hand..."

Julius Fast was an American award winning writer of fiction and non-fiction work dealing especially with human physiology and behaviour. His book *Body Language* was among the first to bring the subject to a mainstream audience.

The exception among Fast's contemporary influences was Charles Darwin, and specifically his book *The Expression of the Emotions in Man and Animals*, written in 1872, which is commonly regarded as the beginnings of the body language science, albeit not recognised as such then.

Sigmund Freud and others in the field of psychoanalysis - in the late 1800s and early 1900s - would have had good awareness of many aspects of body language, including personal space, but they did not focus on non-verbal communications concepts or develop body language theories in their own right. Freud and similar psychoanalysts and psychologists of that time were focused on behaviour and therapeutic analysis rather than the study of non-verbal communications *per se*.

A different view of human behaviour related to and overlapping body language, surfaced strongly in Desmond Morris's 1967 book *The Naked Ape*, and in follow-up books such as Intimate Behaviour, 1971. Morris, a British zoologist and ethologist, linked human behaviour - much of it concerned with communications - to human 'animalistic' evolution. His work remains a popular and controversial perspective for understanding people's behaviours, and while his theories did not focus strongly on body language, Morris's popularity in the late 1960s and 1970s contributed significantly to the increasing interest among people beyond the scientific community - for a better understanding of how and why we feel and act and communicate.

An important aspect of body language is facial expression, which is arguably one part of body language for which quite early 'scientific' thinking can be traced:

- **Physiognomy** is an obscure and related concept to body language. Physiognomy refers to facial features and expressions which were/are said indicate the person's character or nature, or ethnic origin.

  The word physiognomy is derived from medieval Latin, and earlier Greek (*phusiognominia*), which originally meant (the art or capability of) judging a person's nature from his/her facial features and expressions. The ancient roots of this concept demonstrate that while body language itself is a recently defined system of analysis, the notion of inferring human nature or character from facial expression is extremely old.

- **Kinesics** (pronounced 'kineesicks' with stress on the 'ee') is the modern technical word for body language, and more scientifically the study of body language.

  The word kinesics was first used in English in this sense in the 1950s, deriving from the Greek word kinesis, meaning motion, and seems to have first been used by Dr Ray Birdwhistell, an American 1950s researcher and writer on body language.

  The introduction of a new technical word - (in this case, kinesics) - generally comes after the establishment of the subject it describes, which supports the assertion that the modern concept of body language - encompassing facial expressions and personal space - did not exist until the 1950s.

- **Proxemics** is the technical term for the **personal space** aspect of body language. The word was devised in the late 1950s or early 1960s by Edward Twitchell Hall, an American anthropologist. The word is Hall's adaptation of the word proximity, meaning closeness or nearness.

  From the word kinesics, Ray Birdwhistell coined the term **kine** to refer to a single body language signal. This is not to be confused with the ancient and same word kine, meaning a group of cows. Neither word seems to have caught on in a big way, which in one way is a pity, but in another way probably makes matters simpler for anyone interested in the body language of cows.

  Kinaesthetics (also known as kinesthetics) in the study of learning styles, is related to some of the principles of body language, in terms of conveying meaning and information via physical movement and experience.

Body language is among many branches of science and education which seek to interpret and exploit messages and meaning from the 'touchy-feely' side of life.

For example, the concepts of experiential learning, games and exercises, and love and spirituality at work - are all different perspectives and attempts to unlock and develop people's potential using ideas centred around kinaesthetics, as distinct from the more tangible and easily measurable areas of facts, figures words and logic.

BODY LANGUAGE - NATURE OR NURTURE?

Body language is part of human evolution, but as with many other aspects of human behaviour, the precise mixture of genetic (inherited) and environmental (learned or conditioned) influences is not known, and opinions vary.

Julius Fast noted this, especially regarding facial expressions. To emphasise the shifting debate he cited for example:

- Darwin's belief that human facial expressions were similar among humans of all cultures, due to evolutionary theory.
- Bruner and Taguiri's opposing views - in the early 1950s, after thirty years of research, they largely rejected the notion that facial expressions were inborn.
- and Ekman, Friesan and Sorensen's findings - in 1969, having discovered consistent emotional-facial recognition across widely diverse cultural groups, which supported Darwin's evolutionary-centred ideas.

The discussion has continued in a similar vein to the modern day - studies 'proving' genetic or environmental cause - 'nature' or 'nurture' - for one aspect of body language or another.

The situation is made more complex when one considers the genetic (inherited) capability or inclination to learn body language. Is this nature or nurture?

It's both.

Body language is partly genetic (inborn - 'nature') - hugely so in certain aspects of body language - and partly environmental (conditioned/learned - 'nurture').

Some body language is certainly genetically inherited and consistent among all humans. Other body language is certainly not.

The use and recognition of certain fundamental facial expressions are now generally accepted to be consistent and genetically determined among all humans regardless of culture.

However the use and recognition of less fundamental physical gestures (hand movements for example, or the winking of an eye), and aspects of personal space distances, are now generally accepted to be environmentally determined (learned, rather than inherited), which is significantly dependent on local society groups and cultures.

Certain vocal intonation speech variations (if body language is extended to cover everything but the spoken words) also fall within this environmentally determined category.

In summary, we can be certain that body language (namely the conscious and unconscious sending and receiving of non-verbal signals) is partly inborn, and partly learned or conditioned.

BODY LANGUAGE AND EVOLUTION

The evolutionary perspectives of body language are fascinating, in terms of its purpose and how it is exploited, which in turn feeds back into the purpose of body language at conscious and unconscious levels.

Human beings tend to lie, deceive, manipulate, and pretend. It's in our nature to do this, if only to a small degree in some folk.

For various reasons people intentionally and frequently mask their true feelings.

In expectation of these 'masking' tendencies in others, humans try to imagine what another person has in their mind. The need to understand what lies behind the mask obviously increases according to the importance of the relationship.

Body language helps us to manage and guard against these tendencies, and also - significantly especially in flirting/dating/mating rituals - body language often helps people to communicate and resolve relationship issues when conscious behaviour and speech fails to do so.

Body language has evolved in spite of human awareness and conscious intelligence: rather like a guardian angel, body language can help take care of us, connecting us to kindred souls, and protecting us from threats.

While the importance of body language in communications and management, etc., has become a popular interest and science in the last few decades, human beings have relied on body language instinctively in many ways for many thousands of years.

Early natural exponents of interpreting body language were for example the poker players of the American Wild West. The winners had not only to be handy with a six-shooter, but also skilled in reading other people's non-verbal signals, and controlling their own signals.

Before these times, explorers and tribal leaders had to be able to read the body language of potential foes - to know whether to trust or defend or attack.

Earlier than this, our cavemen ancestors certainly needed to read body language, if only because no other language existed.

Humans have also learned to read the body language of animals (and *vice-versa*), although humans almost certainly had greater skills in this area a long time ago. Shepherds, horse-riders and animal trainers throughout time and still today have good capabilities in reading animal body language, which for many extends to the human variety. Monty Roberts, the real life 'Horse Whisperer' is a good example.

Body language, and the reading of non-verbal communications and feelings, are in our genes. Were these factors not in our genes, we would not be here today.

On which point:

Women tend to have better perception and interpretation of body language than men. This is perhaps a feature of evolutionary survival, since females needed good body language skills to reduce their physical vulnerability to males and the consequential threat to life, limb and offspring. Females might not be so physically vulnerable in modern times, but their body language capabilities generally continue typically to be stronger than the male of the species. Thus, women tend to be able to employ body language (for sending and interpreting signals) more effectively than men.

Katherine Benziger's theories of brain types and thinking styles provides useful additional perspective. Women tend to have more empathic sensitivity than men, which naturally aids body language awareness and capabilities. Aside from gender differences, men and women with strong empathic sensitivity (typically right-basal or rear brain bias) tend to be better at picking up body language signals.

THE SIX UNIVERSAL FACIAL EXPRESSIONS

It is now generally accepted that certain basic facial expressions of human emotion are recognized around the world - and that the use and recognition of these expressions is genetically inherited rather than socially conditioned or learned.

While there have been found to be minor variations and differences among obscurely isolated tribes-people, the following basic human emotions are generally used, recognized, and part of humankind's genetic character:

These emotional face expressions are:

- Happiness
- Sadness
- Fear
- Disgust
- Surprise
- Anger

Charles Darwin was first to make these claims in his book The Expressions of the Emotions in Man and Animals, published in 1872. This book incidentally initially far outsold The Origin of Species, such was its wide (and controversial) appeal at the time.

Darwin's assertions about genetically inherited facial expressions remained the subject of much debate for many years.

In the 1960s a Californian psychiatrist and expert in facial expressions, Paul Ekman, conducted and published extensive studies with people of various cultures to explore the validity of Darwin's theory - that certain facial expressions and man's ability to recognize them are inborn and universal among people. Ekman's work notably included isolated tribes-people who could not have been influenced by Western media and images, and essentially proved that Darwin was right - i.e., that the use and recognition of facial expressions to convey certain basic human emotions is part of human evolved nature, genetically inherited, and not dependent on social learning or conditioning.

Body language analysis

Body language is instinctively interpreted by us all to a limited degree, but the subject is potentially immensely complex. Perhaps infinitely so, given that the human body is said to be capable of producing 700,000 different movements.

As with other behavioural sciences, the study of body language benefited from the development of brain-imaging technology in the last part of the 20th century. This dramatically accelerated the research and understanding into connections between the brain, feelings and thoughts, and body movement. We should expect to see this effect continuing and providing more solid science for body language theory, much of which remains empirical, i.e., based on experience and observation, rather than scientific test.

Given the potential for confusion, here are some considerations when analysing body language:

Context

Body language also depends on context: body language in a certain situation might not mean the same in another.

Some 'body language' isn't what it seems at all, for example:

- Someone rubbing their eye might have an irritation, rather than being tired - or disbelieving, or upset.
- Someone with crossed arms might be keeping warm, rather than being defensive.
- Someone scratching their nose might actually have an itch, rather than concealing a lie.

Sufficient samples/evidence

A single body language signal isn't as reliable as several signals:

- As with any system of evidence, 'clusters' of body language signals provide much more reliable indication of meaning than one or two signals in isolation.
- Avoid interpreting only single signals. Look for combinations of signals which support an overall conclusion, especially for signals which can mean two or more quite different things.

Culture/ethnicity

Certain body language is the same in all people, for example smiling and frowning, but some body language is specific to a culture or ethnic group.

Body Language in Different Cultures

Here are some brief pointers concerning body language variations and gestures in cultures which differ from Western (US/UK notably) behaviour.

People in/from parts of India may to shake their head from side to side as a sign of agreement and active listening. In the UK/west we tend to nod our head to agree and affirm and to show we are listening; in India it is not unusual for people to move their heads from side to side in giving these reactions. It is also seen as respectful practice.

This point (thanks R Fox) concerns eye contact. Eye contact (other than unwanted staring) is generally regarded as a positive aspect of body language in Western cultures, which in this context typically refers to white European people and descendents. A specific difference regarding eye contact can be found in some black Caribbean cultures however, whereby young people tend to be instructed not look at someone eye to eye when being told off or disciplined. When cultures meet obviously this provides potential for friction, given the 'Western' expectation in such situations, for example, "Look at me when I'm talking to you".

Filipino people (and in fact many other people of all races) can find it offensive/uncomfortable when beckoned by a repeatedly curled index finger - the gesture evokes feelings of having done something wrong and being chastised for it.

In some Australian Aboriginal cultures, it is disrespectful to look an elder, or person of a rank above you, in the eyes. It is a sign of respect to drop your eyes, (whereas in Western culture not meeting somebody's gaze is commonly considered to be a negative sign, indicating deceit, lying, lack of attention, lack of confidence, etc).

In Arab countries the thumbs-up gesture is rude. Showing the soles of the feet is insulting/rude in many Asian and Arab cultures, especially pointing the foot or feet at anyone. Feet are considered 'inferior' parts of the body compared with the dignity of the face. In Arab culture the left hand and right hands have religious connotations which generally dictate that the left hand is not used for touching (for example shaking hands) or eating. Arab handshaking tends to be more frequent and less firm - on meeting and departing, even several times in the same day.

The eyebrow flash may be considered rude or to carry sexual connotations in Japanese culture. Informal male-female touching is less common and can be considered improper in Japan.

The American-style 'OK' sign - a circle made with thumb and index-finger with other fingers fanned or outstretched - is a rude gesture in some cultures, notably Latin America, Germany and the Middle East.

Beckoning gestures in Eastern cultures are commonly made with the palm down, whereas Western beckoning is generally palm up.

The offensive British/Western two-fingered V-sign is not necessarily offensive in Japan and may be considered positive like the Western palm-outwards 'victory' or 'peace' V-sign in the West.

In some countries, Greece, Turkey and Bulgaria for example, moving the head up/down or from side to side may have additional or different meanings to those conventionally interpreted in the UK/US. Specifically, in Turkey, aside from using conventional (US/UK-style) head nodding and shaking, some people may also signal 'no' by moving their head up.

In Japan the male bow is still commonly used, when the depth of the bow increases with the amount of respect shown, and is therefore a signal of relative status between two people.

In The Netherlands people touch the temple with the index finger in order to indicate someone (or an action) is smart or intelligent. Touching the forehead with the index finger means someone (or an action) is stupid or crazy. In Russia these meanings are reversed.

Here are some Japanese body language insights, especially for doing business in Japan (thanks R Wilkes):

- High-pitched laughter means nervousness.
- On introduction, do not offer a handshake. Depth of bow is impossible to judge without immense experience: it is sufficient for a Westerner to bow shallowly.
- Business cards should be exchanged at the first possible opportunity. The card received should be held in both hands

and examined carefully, and then stored, preferably in a wallet, on the upper half of the body. Holding a person's identity in one hand is casual/disrespectful. The trouser pocket is a rude place.

- Blowing one's nose into a handkerchief in public is obscene. (What other bodily waste do you wrap up in cotton and put in your pocket?..)

- Japanese businesses (unless they cannot afford it) have two types of meeting room: a Western style room with central table, and a room with sofas. The sofa room is for non-antagonistic meetings. In general, the 45 degree rule seems to apply here - better to sit on adjacent sides than across from one another. This room can be a great place to cut deals. Nevertheless, the 'table' room is where transactions are formalised. There the host of the meeting sits nearest to (and preferably with his back to) the door. (This is probably chivalric in origin - he is first in the way of any invader to the room.) His team sits on the same side of the table in descending rank. The chief guest sits opposite him and similarly the minions decline to the side. The head of the table is not generally used in bilateral (two parties) meetings except by people brought in to advise on components of the agenda. A great boss may spend much of the meeting with his eyes closed. He is considering what is being said by the subordinates and does not need visual distraction. However, if he has a firm steer to give, he will instruct his deputy and this will be relayed immediately.

- Loss of eye contact is quite normal with lower ranking people: if they drop their head, this indicates deep thought.

- Otherwise, pure body signals are quite similar to Western ones, with one notable exception: touching the tip of the nose from straight ahead signals 'I/me'.

- The Japanese language does have a word for 'no' but it is rarely used in business for fear of causing offence or loss of face. "Yes, but..." is substantially more acceptable.

Awareness of possible cultural body language differences is especially important in today's increasingly mixed societies.

Management and customer service staff are particularly prone to misreading or reacting inappropriately to body language signals from people of different ethnic backgrounds, a situation made worse because this sort of misunderstanding tends to peak when emotions are high.

Personal space preferences (distances inside which a person is uncomfortable when someone encroaches) can vary between people of different ethnicity.

In general this article offers interpretations applicable for Western culture.

BODY LANGUAGE IS RELATIVE TO AGE AND GENDER

Many body language signals are relative.

A gesture by one person in a certain situation can carry far more, or very little meaning, compared to the same gesture used by a different person in a different situation.

Young men for example often display a lot of pronounced gestures because they are naturally energetic, uninhibited and supple. Older women, relatively, are less energetic, adopt more modest postures, and are prevented by clothing and upbringing from exhibiting very pronounced gestures.

So when assessing body language - especially the strength of signals and meanings - it's important to do so in relative terms, considering the type of person and situation involved.

FAKING/DECEPTION

Some people artificially control their outward body language to give the impression they seek to create at the time.

A confident firm handshake, or direct eye contact, are examples of signals which can be quite easily be 'faked' - usually temporarily, but sometimes more consistently.

However while a degree of faking is possible, it is not possible for someone to control or suppress all outgoing signals.

This is an additional reason to avoid superficial analysis based on isolated signals, and to seek as many indicators as possible, especially subtle clues when suspecting things might not be what they seem. Politicians and manipulative salespeople come to mind for some reason.

Looking for 'micro gestures' (pupils contract, an eyebrow lifts, corner of the mouth twitch) can help identify the true meaning and motive behind one or two strong and potentially false signals.

These micro gestures are very small, difficult to spot and are subconscious, but we cannot control them, hence their usefulness.

BOREDOM, NERVOUSNESS AND INSECURITY SIGNALS

Many body language signals indicate negative feelings such as boredom, disinterest, anxiousness, insecurity, etc.

The temptation on seeing such signals is to imagine a weakness on the part of the person exhibiting them.

This can be so, however proper interpretation of body language should look beyond the person and the signal - and consider the situation, especially if you are using body language within personal development or management. Ask yourself:

- What is causing the negative feelings giving rise to the negative signals?

It is often the situation, not the person - for example, here are examples of circumstances which can produce negative feelings and signals in people, often even if they are strong and confident:

- dominance of a boss or a teacher or other person perceived to be in authority
- overloading a person with new knowledge or learning
- tiredness

- stress caused by anything
- cold weather or cold conditions
- lack of food and drink
- illness or disability
- alcohol or drugs
- being in a minority or feeling excluded
- unfamiliarity - newness - change

Ask yourself, when analysing body language:

- Are there external factors affecting the mood and condition of the individual concerned?
- Do not jump to conclusions - especially negative ones - using body language analysis alone.

BODY LANGUAGE - TRANSLATION OF GESTURES, SIGNS AND OTHER FACTORS

When translating body language signals into feelings and meanings remember that one signal does not reliably indicate a meaning.

Clusters of signals more reliably indicate meaning.

This is a general guide. Body language should not be used alone for making serious decisions about people.

Body language is one of several indicators of mood, meaning and motive.

This is a guide, not an absolutely reliable indicator, and this applies especially until you've developed good capabilities of reading body language signs.

Some of these signs have obvious meanings; others not so.

Even 'obvious' signs can be missed - especially if displayed as subtle movements in a group of people and if your mind is on other things - so I make no apology for including 'obvious' body language in this guide.

Also remember that cultural differences influence body language signals and their interpretation. This guide is based on 'Western World' and North European behaviours. What may be 'obvious' in one culture can mean something different in another culture.

body language signs translation

The body language signals below are grouped together according to parts of the body.

Left and right are for the person giving the signals and making the movements.

This is a summary of the main body language signals. More signals and meanings will be added.

Postures and positions

There is no word as clear as body language, once one has learned to read it.

Psychological attitudes are said to affect the posture and the functioning of the body, in such a way that neurotic problems also become apparent in the body's structure and function. If body language reveals an individual's state of mind, personality and ability to establish contact with others, it should be possible for the individual to change by modifying his body language. The important thing is to understand the message he is trying to transmit and what he is really saying with the different parts of his body.

A person who knows about body language and how to use it has learned to master the most important postures and can associate them with emotional states. Such a person will be more perceptive when dealing with others. It is an art that can be taught, since it depends on careful observation, but it is only learned if one is aware that it exists.

Remember that

- A round-shouldered person cannot have the strong ego of a person who keeps his back straight; on the other hand, a straight-backed person will be less flexible.
- Hunched shoulders mean contained annoyance; raised shoulders are associated with fear; wide, straight shoulders denote assuming responsibilities; drooping shoulders have the connotation of carrying a heavy burden.

Movements of the head, eyelids, and hands do not represent different postures but they are called points. A sequence of several points is qualified as a position, which involves at least half of the body and can last almost five minutes.

Bear in mind that:

- When holding a conversation, people use certain head movements to indicate that they have come to the end of a sentence and are waiting for the other person's answer.
- When talking, men and women normally look right and left, up and down; they blink; they raise their eyebrows; bite their lips; touch their nose. Each movement is linked to what they are saying. Just as lowering the head indicates thc cnd of a statement or raising the head the end of a question, major modifications in posture indicate ending points in interpretations.

Posture is not only a means of punctuating conversation, it is also the way in which people relate to each other when they are together. Three types of postures are distinguished:

- inclusive or non inclusive
- face-to-face or parallel
- congruent or incongruent.

Inclusive or Non-inclusive

Inclusivity or non-inclusivity refers to the way in which the members of a group include people or fail to include them. They do it by positioning their bodies, arms, or legs in a certain way. The arms and legs of the members of the group are unconsciously used to protect the group from intrusion.

Face-to-face or Parallel

The second category assumes that two persons can relate with each other in terms of posture, face-to-face, sitting beside each, other or maybe facing toward a third person. The face-to-face position is usual in a teacher-student relationship or a doctor-patient relationship where emotions or information are being transmitted.

Parallel positions occur, for example, among two or more students listening to a teacher. Parallel arrangements, when freely adopted, indicate that those persons are probably in a neutral situation, at least at that moment.

The way a couple position themselves in a social gathering also says a great deal about their relationship.

Congruent or Incongruent

This category refers to the ability of the members of a group to imitate each other.

When a group is in congruence, the positions of their bodies mimic each other, in some cases like mirror images.

Interestingly, when one member of a congruent group changes his position, everyone does so with him. The congruence of position of a group usually indicates that all the members are in agreement. If the group has two points of view, the defenders of each opinion will adopt different positions; each subgroup will be congruent within itself, but not congruent with the other subgroup. The leader in any social or family gathering often selects the position for the group and they all invariably follow him or her.

The parts of the body and body language

The different parts of the body constantly communicate people's state of mind, personality, and attitude. For example, the dominant person plants his feet squarely on the ground, adopts a firm posture, and sometimes uses bullying tactics, all of which expresses control over his affairs and responsibility for them. On the other hand, the use of too many body movements without any real significance is associated with immature personalities.

The following paragraphs summarize what can be expressed by different parts of the body, such as the hands or the face, and associated aspects, such as clothing and timing.

The Hands

Hands have a very important role to play in communications. Their movement is closely associated with the emotions. When a person wants to emphasize or stress his words, he makes his hand movements bigger and more deliberate.

Bear in mind that:

- In Latin countries, every statement is accompanied by ample movements of the arms and hands, unlike Saxon countries where people make more limited movements.
- If we observe a young man waiting for his fiancée, we can perceive whether he is anxious, grieved, fearful or confident by the way he moves, joins his hands, or keeps them close to his body. We can even glimpse what he expects from that encounter.

Hand movements are more frequent when a person is having difficulty expressing his ideas verbally or when it is difficult for him to make himself understood. The greater his need to make himself understood, the greater intensity he will give to the expression of his hands and he will gesticulate more amply.

Interest or concern about an issue can be hinted at by touching the forearm of the other person. Also, with a handshake in certain situations it is possible to reveal and capture the most varied feelings of strength or weakness, attitudes of superiority or inferiority, enthusiasm or coldness, interest or lack of interest, confidence or insecurity, fear, or anxiety.

Remember that:

- When expressing condolences, we often do this with a warm handshake and a gentle hug; sorrow is transmitted in this way more naturally and effectively than with words.
- The greeting that follows visual contact is a demonstration of dominance. If we shake hands firmly and enthusiastically, we are giving the message that we possess sufficient strength and amiability to control the situation. On the other hand, a weak handshake suggests the kind of person who prefers to keep his distance and reserve his social space, someone who is enclosed within himself.

The Eyes

Of all the parts of the human body used to transmit information, the eyes are the most capable of reflecting very fine nuances. The first contact we make with a person is usually through the eyes; and one look is often enough to start or end a relationship, to choose or reject a person.

The eye muscles are so wonderfully subtle that one look can differ minutely from another; and tell us what is going on inside the person who is looking. Also, communication with one's eyes is more revealing when it is done unconsciously.

There are different formulae for exchanging looks, depending on where the meeting occurs. Sometimes we use the technique of looking-and-looking-away-again when we meet famous people. We want to reassure them that we respect their privacy.

The same is true when we meet handicapped people or invalids: we look at them briefly and then look away to make sure they don't think we are staring at them. In fact, this is the technique we use in any unusual circumstance, when a stare would produce discomfort.

A subtle measurement of time is used when talking, listening, looking, and looking away. Most people look away immediately before or after having pronounced one of each four sentences. Some do so at the beginning or half-way through the sentence.

When they finish speaking, half of the people look at the person they are talking to.

To look away during a conversation can be a means of hiding something. We must remember, however, that the context determines the meaning of people's looks. Visual contact can also modify a relationship. We feel how important the look is when a person refuses to look us in the eye and we cannot perceive whether we interest that person or whether the message we want to transmit is of interest to him or her.

Bear in mind that:

- If we catch someone looking at us, we feel uncomfortable as if there were something wrong. We feel disturbed and annoyed.
- Looking away is associated with the intention to hide the intensity of an emotion or a feeling.
- An absence of visual contact sometimes gives the impression of isolation.
- Strong displeasure is communicated by deliberately avoiding the eyes of the other person or by giving him/her a hard, intense look.

The Face

The expression on a person's face can make a significant difference to the meaning of a message. If we want to send a warm or positive message, we back it up with a friendly smile. If it is a serious message, we show a serious, solemn or cautious expression.

With facial movements we can express a whole range of emotions, from the deepest to the most superficial. If something is bothering us, our annoyance is reflected in a hard or angry facial expression. Happiness is expressed with a change of gesture and with a soft mobility of the facial muscles. An angry person's facial muscles are tense and rigid.

This aspect of body language is very important because our face reveals our thoughts, feelings, and emotions, and our attitudes to people, ideas, or facts. Many people interpret or judge us from our facial expressions.

The human face has a tremendous variety of expressions. If we consider the head as well as the face, we find another whole set of movements. You can nod your head, shake it, turn it away, and raise it sharply; all these movements are significant. However they have different meanings when combined with different facial expressions and in different cultural contexts. The knowledge that people raise their eyebrows or lower their eyelids to express a specific emotion is the result of observation.

The Arms and Legs

We should not read a meaning into the way a person crosses his/her arms and legs, without first taking into account the physiological condition of the person's body. Nevertheless, there is a strong tendency to attribute a series of meanings to the direction in which we cross our arms.

It has apparently been established that crossing one's arms is sometimes a defensive gesture, a sign that one does not accept the point of view of another person, or a lack of security. These and other interpretations are valid, but when we come to the direction of the crossing of arms – left over right, or vice-versa – we are on shakier ground. The difficulty here is that the way we cross our arms is an innate genetic trait, like being right-handed or left-handed.

Prejudices

In daily social interactions, "perceptive selectivity" is expressed in a great many attitudes. This typically means that we perceive the negative aspects of individuals for whom we feel aversion, while we perceive the favorable aspects of those who attract us.

This selective attitude is also clearly manifested in prejudices. Those who prejudge specific social groups observe only those manifestations that agree with their distorted viewpoint and remove from their awareness anything that may run counter to their appraisal.

Body language plays a significant role in selective perception, since all the acts a person performs in our sight will be modified by the opinion we have formed of him, without even knowing him.

Articles and Clothing

The articles people use or have around them reveal things about them. The choice of clothes and accessories tell us about the preferences, the personality, the activities and status of the people wearing them. It is also true that the interpretation of such choices reveals aspects of the personality of the perceiver.

The way we handle objects when we communicate becomes a body language message: how we fidget with a pen, the telephone wire, a salt shaker, a ring, etc. This fidgeting with objects can express nervousness, boredom, lack of interest, anxiety, or other emotions.

Here again we see the need to manage an image in keeping with each personality and the need to make sure that the message we send to individuals or groups is a positive one, so that the response we elicit from them will be equally effective.

Timing

Timing is another element in non-verbal communication. A person's use of time hints at his or her interests, habits and motivations, and says a lot about that person's selfcontrol in specific situations.

If somebody always arrives at his workplace in good time, he is demonstrating interest, responsibility, and companionship. If he is one of those people who arrive late every day, this reveals irresponsibility, bad habits, lack of respect toward his work colleagues, low personal ambition, or excessive self-esteem.

If the time he spends at work explaining a process, giving indications to a colleague or new instructions to a subordinate is adequate, this shows the kind of person he is and the good relationships and positive attitudes he is aiming for. If, on the contrary, he does things hastily and tries to finish as soon as possible, this suggests that he has little interest and more than a little selfishness. The disinterested use of time is always admired by everyone.

CHAPTER 5

Facial Expressions

Unless you're a spy for a foreign country, you probably have never taken a formal course on how to have expert control over your nonverbal communication, or body language. Maybe you will want to, however, after you've learned just how important body language can be in reading someone's message and how much it can truly "give away" one's real feelings and emotions on a subject.

It would be handy to have this basic information when conversing with others. Imagine being able to tell when your partner is interested in what you're saying, open to ideas you have, distracted by other things, or completely bored! That kind of power in a conversation is rarely seen (except by moms and teachers catching children doing mischievous things around the world). If you had insight as to some of the habits of body language and the accompanying facial expressions that are used, you could know the secret language of nonverbal communication. It's almost magic!

During research on body language, people who have had their communication videotaped during various conversations have been shocked to find that they will sometimes accompany a statement with a negative indication through their body language. For example, they might say "yes" with their words, and unconsciously shake their head "no" at the exact same time. Which message is the one they are trying to send? Researchers suggest that while these instances communicate one message consciously, there is always another more subtle message that may enhance, emphasize, or disagree with the spoken statement.

If you're a public speaker, or even just in a casual conversation, your character while communicating will be judged largely by your facial expressions while you talk. Take the simple gesture of a wink, for example. When someone winks at you, it can either evoke a comfortable, warm, friendly feeling or a creepy, lecherous, icky feeling, depending on the facial expression and statements that accompany it. The expressions of the eyes play an enormous role in how our message is received by others.

It has been said the eyes are the windows to our soul. No other part of your facial expression is more important to communicate sincerity and credibility. Making eye contact is one of the most important elements in genuinely sincere conversation. However, as we all know, you don't want to feel like someone is staring you down! Constant eye contact can feel forced or unwelcome and actually do more harm to your message than good.

Effective speakers will engage one individual at a time in eye contact, make a statement clearly, watch for a response, and move on. This practice can put a high amount of energy and enthusiasm into a speaker's presentation, making them seem lively and passionate about their message. Making eye contact on occasion can also insert brief pauses into your side of the conversation. These natural pauses to occasionally sweep the audience with eye focus also encourage audience participation, attentiveness, and allow the topic to really "sink in." The movement of your eyes in conjunction with your mouth and facial muscles can build a connection with the person you're talking to. For example, have you ever gotten the feeling that someone was a trustworthy person after meeting them briefly for the first time? You might have felt this connection with them because of the way their speech was punctuated with pleasant facial expressions or a bright smile. People will judge your communication based in part on the use of your nonverbal cues, so it's important to know what the signals are and how to properly incorporate them into your everyday communication.

However, any facial expression can be taken to the extreme. If you're purchasing a car, for example, and the salesperson has a goofy grin locked onto his face, you're not going to take that person very seriously and will probably leave without buying the car he's selling. There's just something we humans don't trust about a person that smiles too much. Maybe it means they have something to hide or they aren't being exactly honest with us.

Many fear speaking in a group, or may be hesitant to even talk one-on-one! Your nervousness is going to show through in your facial expressions if you aren't careful. Under the pressure of public speaking, many people simply find themselves blank-faced with no facial expression whatsoever. This type of stone statue body language might send the wrong impression that you either don't care much for your subject, or worse yet, your audience!

Try to unfreeze your face when you're speaking by making an initial smile, or raising your eyebrows after the person you're talking with has made an interesting point. Nod your head, furrow your eyebrows; just do something to make sure your face doesn't solidify into a non-existent expression or what I like to call a NONVERBAL LOCKDOWN. Practice makes perfect when learning to control your facial expressions during a conversation, so take a look in the mirror or use a buddy to help you work on yours. You'll feel more confident and project that confidence in no time!

CHAPTER 6

Importance of Body Language in Personality Development

Body language, which is best defined as a non-verbal form of communication showed through facial expressions, gestures, posture, and body movements, says a lot about one's personality. In essence, if you want to achieve an effective personality, you will also need to improve your body language.

There are many ways you can improve your body language, but like most things, it needs practice and consistency so that it will become part of you, and not just something you can do for a certain period of time. If you want to develop your personality in a positive way, you need to be aware of your own body language and make sure it adheres to what is generally perceived as positive body language.

BASIC DO'S FOR BODY LANGUAGE

These are just some of the different body language examples that you should follow.

Maintaining eye contact is a sign of respect and interest towards the other person. If someone is talking and you make sure you are keeping your eyes focused on them then this will make them feel that you are in fact interested in what they have to say.

Another body language is your facial expression. If you are always frowning, this would indicate that you have a negative aura, and this will push others away. Whereas if you are constantly seen smiling, you are going to attract other sunny and happy people to you.

Posture is also very important. You need to sit properly, avoid slouching, and if you can, keep an open posture at all times, leaning towards the speaker whenever necessary, to show that you are interested.

DON'TS FOR BODY LANGUAGE

Just as there are various body language movements and expressions you need to have, there are also those you need to do away with. These kinds of body language are negative, and not at all helpful in projecting a pleasant or winning personality.

- ***Fidgeting***. This would only indicate nervousness and will make the other person doubt your credibility or your ability.
- ***Standing too close***. When you are too close to someone, physically, it will make the other person uncomfortable and will also trigger them to think you are invading their personal space.

- ***Staring***. Though it may not always be the case, staring is considered rude. While you maintain eye contact towards the other person, do not overdo it to the point of staring.

- ***Crossing your arms***. This would indicate resistance on your part, so if someone is talking to you and you are crossing your arms, you will make the other person think that you really are not agreeing to what they have to say and you are making it known to them.

PRACTICE MAKES PERFECT

As mentioned earlier, it is recommended that you keep practicing in order for these body languages to become natural for you. Now that you are already aware of the do's and don'ts, you can easily figure out which ones you need to get used to and which ones you need to get rid of. And little by little, on a daily basis, you need to practice and maintain good body language. Constantly remind yourself of what gestures, movements, and expressions you should have until it will be innate in you.

Your personality can be molded into what you have always wanted. You can attain a winning personality which everyone will admire you for. While you can always work on the way you verbally communicate, improve your confidence, and build a positive aura around you, you also need to be aware of your own body language. Look at yourself in the mirror while you talk and notice every form of body language you portray. Are these positive? If there are those that you do not like, make an effort to eliminate them.

Great speakers are not born, they are made. Before they became great speakers, they underwent a rather difficult process of honing their skills, talents, and yes, even their personality. You too can become one as long as you are committed and geared towards self-improvement. It is not an easy feat, but it is possible, nonetheless.

- Personality Development Tips

- Self Awareness

- Subconscious Mind Programming
- Conscious Mind Programming
- How to Control Your Mind
- Importance of Time in Personality Development
- Importance of Body Language in Personality Development
- Importance of Speech in Personality Development
- Importance of Behavior in Personality Development
- Importance of Character in Personality Development
- Why Personality Development is Important
- How to Avoid Negative Thoughts
- How to Enhance Your Personality
- How to Develop Positive Personality
- Know Your Personality
- Different Personality Types
- Components and Aspects of Our Personality
- What is Personality?

HAND AND ARMS GESTURES

Interestingly, the **hands and arms** are often employed by humans, either knowingly or unknowingly, to express many feelings, which can say a lot about the state of the human psyche.

For instance, we often see many people rubbing the palms of their hands at what time they expect something good to occur. The waiters at restaurants will often rub their palms in expectation of some tip or reward. Although we do it waiting for a delicious meal, the waiters have different intentions, which all boils down to the same thing. Rubbing thumbnails against an index finger is one of the most common signs of asking for money.

When a person loosely clenched his or her hands, it often indicates his/her confidence and relaxed state of mind. Tightly clenched hands on the other hand (no pun intended!) reveal that a person is frustrated or has a hostile attitude. Contextwise, loosely clenched hands in front of the facial area or on the table may reveal that a positive state of mind is in focus, whereas tightly held hands below the stomach area may represent that the person is negatively thinking.

Many people have an I-know-it-all attitude, which could be observed by the way their palms are oriented. The corresponding fingers of both palms touching the other palm, which forms a kind of triangle with their thumbs, and index finger, may represent the know it all attitude. These sort of people are those generally who like to bark out orders to other people. At what time the palms are facing upwards could be a clear indication that the person has an I-know-it-all attitude. As opposed to the, at what time the same shape is formed, but facing downwards, it indicates that the person is willing to listen and take orders.

Gripping Hands, Arms, and Wrists

High-ranking officials like the principal of a school or military and police officials etc. are often seen walking with their head up, chin out and one palm gripping the other behind their back. This gesture signifies superiority and confidence. A person walking in this manner often exposes his stomach, chest, and throat region to others, which is an act of fearlessness. Adopting such a gesture in a stress situation helps a person feel more at ease. This will also boost your confidence. Similarly, palm-in-palm gesture and hands on hips indicate superiority and confidence.

Thumb Gestures

These are probably some of the most commonly observable gestures. We show a raised thumb to say 'all the best' or 'do well' to a person. On the other hand, a thumb facing in the downward direction indicates insult or failure.

Arms Gestures

When a person folds his/her arms about the chest firmly, a feeling of being threatened may exist, since most people may use this gesture as a defensive manouver. This gesture signifies a nervous, negative, or defensive attitude. In addition, when combined with crossed legs posture, it indicates that the person is very tense.

People also fold arms by keeping their thumbs out to indicate superiority. While a folded arms gesture with one palm outside and the other firmly placed between the other arm and the chest may indicate a confused state of mind. In addition, some people fold their arms while keeping their fists firmly clenched to indicate hostility.

The partiallly crossed arm gesture in which one arm swings across the body to hold or to touch the other arm to form a barrier is often made by a person when he/she finds himself/herself lacking in confidence. Holding both your palms just below the stomach can mean that the person either is trying to de-stress himself or is in a position where he has to take orders from someone.

Arm Shields

Humans as defensive mechanisms have always had the need to hide behind something in search for protection. With children it was behind tables, chairs or our parents if we saw a scary looking dog, but around 7 we knew hiding wasn't possible anymore, so we would cross our arms quite tightly when throwing tantrums. In our adolescence we'd cross our arms more subtly and also combine this defensive gesture with crossing our legs and finally, as adults, we've found even less obvious ways of giving us that security and protection we so badly crave.

Crossed Arms

This is when the arms are neatly folded across the chess to protect the heart, lungs and other vital organs as well as breasts in most womens cases. We will usually cross our arms when we feel nervous, negative towards something/someone or are feeling defensive (such as when someone is making fun of our top/ dress and we cross our arms in response). Monkeys have also been observed to do the exact same gesture when they feel they are in a threatening situation. You can commonly see the crossed arm gesture in public meetings amongst strangers, elevators, cashier shopping lines or any place where we feel insecure or uncertain of our surroundings.

Crossed Arms With Fists

If, as well as crossing their arms, the person has clenched fists as well, this is a strong sign of hostility. This combined gesture is an aggressive and attacking attitude that you should watch out for. This gesture is often times found in jobs that require hostility and defensiveness, such as bouncers or police men standing guard (patrolling policemen rarely cross their arms as they have a weapon for protection, which is enough. The same goes for anyone wearing a body armor, they'll never cross their arms).

Self-Reassurance Cross

This gesture is when someone crosses their arms while tightly grabbing their biceps or elbows. The self-reassurance cross is a display of a fearful, negative, restrained or insecure attitude. Ever wondered where the fetus position came from? It's the ultimate act of physical self reassurance whereby we use our knees and legs to protect our vital organs and body locking our tightly held position with our arms and lowering our vulnerable neck (predators went for our necks). You can commonly find such self reassuring gestures in hospital/doctor waiting rooms, airport lounges with first time travelers or defendants at court room hearings.

Arm Crossed With Thumbs

The displaying the thumbs is the sign of a superior or self confident attitude. This gesture can often be seen in situations when someone is feeling they are cool and in control while still maintaining a level of protection with the crossed arms just in case. This can also be seen in exams for instance, where the student feels confident about his abilities to answer correctly yet still feels a bit threatened by something going wrong.

One Crossed Arm

This type of body shield is a single arm crossing the chest and grabbing or touching the bicep or elbow of the opposite arm. As young children our parents would embrace or hug us when we were going through distressful moments, so as adults we try to recreate that same comforting feeling by doing it ourselves. This action resembles a self hug and is more popular amongst woman than men. You can also often find this arm gesture in social group situations where one of the individuals is a stranger to the group and feels a lack self confidence.

Self Holding Hands

This type of arm gesture is the male version of the predominantly female 'One Crossed Arm' gesture mentioned above, and is used by men who are insecure or lack self confidence in a certain situation. You can find this pose in some men who are awaiting to speak in front of a big crowd and are nervous, at funerals, and can also be observed in homeless men standing in line to await a plate of food or to receive a social security benefit. This arm gesture is also popular among men who feel the need to protect their "Family Jewels" as a form of security to unconsciously avoid receiving a frontal blow. More obvious examples of this are soccer players making a barrier in front of a free shot from the opposite team. Adolf Hitler only had one testicle so he regularly adopted this position (or at least with only one arm protecting the jewels) when in public to mask the sexual inadequacy he felt.

Subtle Arm Crosses

People of high status such as politicians, celebrities or people in high positions can't afford to look nervous or unsure about themselves as they are constantly in the limelight - they can't walk around crossing their arms or walk around with their hands in front of their crotch, so instead, they choose subtler ways of crossing arms and achieve that secure feeling once more. Men will go for things like adjusting their watches or shirt cufflinks, to fiddling with their ring if they have one, scratching their wrists, checking inside their wallets or looking at their mobile phones, or anything that brings the arms in front of the body when they feel nervous and in full view of others (e.g. entering parties, new crowds, walking through wedding dance floors, etc.) Women however have a bigger advantage as they often carry accessories for when they feel self conscious or insecure. Many women use their purse as a barrier for instance. Women also have more jewelry to 'adjust' and fiddle around with. At clubs for instance, you can notice that some people hold their drinks with two hands instead of one - unless it's a cold winters night and the cup has some warm tea, this action is rather pointless. A popular arm gesture that men and women do alike is when sitting at a table opposite of you, they may place their glass/ cup on the opposite side of the arm they use to move it - this way, they have to cross one arm in front of their body to reach it and can remain with their arms crossed in front of you while touching the glass.

LIPS BODY LANGUAGE

Lips can say a lot of things without words. Our muscles around them mean we can shape them with incredibly fine control. Lipstick is used to draw attention to the lips, thus exaggerating further the signals sent by them.

Parted

Lips which are slightly parted can be a strong flirting signal, particularly if the lips are then licked and even more so if done whilst holding the gaze of another person.

Parting lips is the first stage in speaking and may thus be a signal that the person wants to talk.

Pursed

Lips which are pulled inwards from all directions are an indication of tension and may indicate frustration or disapproval.

Pursed lips are a classic sign of anger, including when it is suppressed. It is effectively holding the mouth shut to prevent the person saying what they feel like saying. This may also be an indication of lying or withholding the truth as the person stops themselves from telling the truth.

Pursed lips can also indicate a person who is thinking and who is deciding between possible options. Deciding and disapproval are both evaluative actions, which is the common core of lip-pursing.

Puckered

A light puckering of the lips into a kiss shape typically indicates desire. It can also indicate uncertainty, particularly if the lips are touched with the fingers.

When you say 'oo', the lips form the kiss shape. This is one reason that romantic songs often linger on words like 'you' and 'too'.

Sucked in

When lips are sucked into the mouth or turned under so the red part of the lips are hidden ('swallowing the lips'), this can indicate that the person is thinking and uncertain about something, which could easily be bad news.

Lip swallowing can also indicate suppressed speech, where the person is preventing themself from speaking when perhaps they know they should. This can indicate lying or maybe disapproval.

Flattened

Lips which are kept horizontal but squeezed flat are an exaggerated closing of the mouth (hence the name 'lip press') and may indicate a repressed desire to speak. This indicate disapproval

('If I spoke I would be very critical, which I do not want to be'). It can also indicate frustration ('I want to speak, but others are speaking and I feel I should wait').

Flattened lips can also indicate a refusal to eat, either because of dislike of offered food or some other motivation.

Another possibility is distress, where the person is trying not to cry or turn down their mouth in sadness.

Turned up

When the corners of the mouth are turned upwards, this can be a grimace of disgust or a smile of pleasure. In a grimace, the teeth are unlikely to be shown (although toothless smiles are also common). Grimaces are often flatter and tenser.

A full smile engages the whole face, particularly including the eyes. Smiling with lips only is often falsehood, where the smiler wants to convey pleasure or approval but is actually feeling something else.

Turned down

Corners of the mouth turned down indicates sadness or displeasure.

Some people are so miserable so often, this is the natural state of rest of their mouths (which is perhaps rather sad).

Retracted

When the lips are pulled back, they expose the teeth. This may be in a broad smile or it may be a snarl of aggression. The eyes should tell you which is which. In a snarl, the eyes are either narrowed or staring. In a full smile, the corners of the eyes are creased.

Moving

Lips which are moving in the shape of words but without making sounds means that the person is thinking of saying the words. This subvocalization often happens with very small movement and is often completely subconscious. Stage mentalists use this when they ask their 'victims' to think hard of a word and then lip-read as they silently sound the word.

Up and down movement may indicate chewing. Some people chew the insides of their mouths when they are nervous.

Rolling in the lips so they roll across one another can be a preening gesture for women, evening out lipstick. It can also be a sign of uncertainty or disapproval (look for accompanying lowered eyebrows).

Twitching

Small, lightning-fast movements of the mouth betray inner thoughts, for example a single twitch of the corner of the mouth that indicates cynicism or disbelief.

Liars in particular will often give themselves away with very brief grimaces as their conscience expresses disapproval of the conscious lies.

Protruding

When the top lip is over the bottom lip, this may be linked with biting of the bottom lip, a common indicator that the person is feeling guilty about something.

The bottom lip extended over the top lip can indicate uncertainty, as if the person is saying 'umm'.

The bottom lip jutting out is often a part of a sulky pout, where the person expresses child-like petulance at not getting their own way.

Both lips pressed together and pushed out generally indicates doubt. If the finger touches them, it may indicate internal thinking or may say 'I am considering speaking but am not quite ready to talk yet'.

Biting

Biting the lip, centrally or at the side, is often a sign of anxiety. Usually, this is the bottom lip (especially if the person has overhanging top teeth). This may be a habitual action and people who do this, will often repeat the move in predictable situations. It can also be an indicator for stress during lying.

This is a fairly child-like action, especially if accompanied by wide eyes and eyebrows raised in the middle and lowered at the sides, and thus may betray concern about being told off or otherwise being censured in the manner of a child.

As well as a comforting action, biting the lip can be a suppressing action as a person is stopping themself from saying something.

Relaxed

Finally, the lips will have a position of rest when they are not pulled in any direction. This usually indicates that the person is also feeling relaxed.

MOUTH BODY LANGUAGE

Generally speaking body orifices are not terribly desirable as they can cause problems such as being entries for disease or can be snagged on passing bushes. The mouth is perhaps the ultimate multi-function orifice as we use it for communicating, breathing and eating.

Emoting

The mouth is involved in the expression of many different emotions, from happiness to sadness, from fear to disgust. In emoting, the lips play a major role in creating visible shapes, with able backup from the teeth and tongue.

Studies have shown that people who are good at identifying emotions tend to watch the other person's mouth more than their eyes, as has previously been thought.

Breathing

We usually breath through the nose, but when we need more oxygen we use the mouth to gulp in greater amounts of air.

A person who is frightened or angry by the fight-or-flight reaction may well open their mouth to get more oxygen in preparation for combat or running away. This may also involve breathing faster (panting).

Stressed breathing may even include gulping air and blowing it out. At worst a person may hyperventilate, breathing too fast and becoming dizzy, even to the point of collapse.

A hot person also pants hard. With typical the red face, this can be mistaken for anger (or vice versa).

Yawning is a process of taking a deep gulp of air as a quick 'pick-me-up' and often indicate a person who is tired or bored.

A short, deep, exhaling sigh, can indicate sadness, frustration or boredom.

Short inhalation, particularly in a sequence, can be like silent sobs and hence be an indicator of deep and suppressed sadness.

Slow, deep breathing, sometimes with slightly parted lips, may indicate someone who is relaxing or meditating. With closed eyes, they are seldom aware of what is going on around them and this may be done as an escape.

Speaking

The mouth sends additional signals when it is speaking.

If the mouth moves little, perhaps including incoherent mumbling, this may indicate an unwillingness to speak, for example from shyness or from a fear of betraying themselves.

A mouth that moves a lot during speech can indicate excitement or dominance as it sends clear signals that 'I am speaking, do not interrupt!'

Careful shaping of words can also indicate a person with auditory preferences or a concern for precision and neatness.

Fast speakers are often visual thinkers who are trying to get out what they are seeing. They may also be looking upwards.

Slow speakers may be deep thinkers who are being careful about finding the right words. They may also have an auditory preference as they carefully enunciate each word.

Eating

The mouth is also used for eating, and the way people eat can tell things about them.

A well-mannered person opens their mouth the minimum to put in a moderate amount of food and keeps it closed whilst carefully chewing each mouthful. They also do not speak when they have food in their mouth.

On the other hand, an uncouth person gobbles large mouthfuls and opens their mouth as they chew and talk at the same time.

In a curious reversal, snobbish gourmands who take great pleasure in eating may do it noisily as an expression of pleasure. This may also be a cultural variable and in some places noisy eating is not only acceptable but also desirable.

People who chew smaller amounts at the front of their mouth are like children whose molars have not developed and may be timid.

People who chew for a longer time may be chewing on ideas at the same time.

When people slide their jaw sideways when they eat are grinding the food. this may also be pensive.

Drinking

As with eating, drinking may be done in a polite way, sipping smaller amounts and swallowing noiselessly. It may also be done with loud glugging and followed by equally distasteful burping — although again, in some cultures this is a desirable expression of pleasure.

Someone who is slooshing their drink around their mouth may well be thinking and deciding.

Covering

Sometimes the hand is used to cover the mouth. In polite society, exposing the inside of your mouth may be considered rude, so the hand is used to politely cover a yawn.

The hand is also used to conceal the mouth when it will betray emotions that may be undesirable. Thus we put our hands over impolite giggles and smirks, and we may do this to hold back from telling the truth.

Covering the mouth may also be a reason for hiding a yawn. We also cover the open mouth of surprise and the downturned mouth of sadness.

Smiling

Smiling indicates pleasure, either that you are generally happy and are enjoying the other person's company or that you are amused by something in particular, such as a joke.

A full smile engages the whole face, particularly including the eyes, which crease and 'twinkle'. A true smile is also known as the Duchenne smile, after the scientists who first described it in 1862. False smiles also tend to last for longer.

Smiling with lips only is often falsehood, where the smiler wants to convey pleasure or approval but is actually feeling something else. Long, tense smiles are characteristic of anxious people trying to ingratiate themselves ('Don't hurt me — I'm nice!').

A genuine smile is often asymmetric and usually larger on the right side of the face. A false smile may be more symmetrical or larger on the left side of the face.

Lowering the jaw to show a D-shaped mouth can be a false smile as it is easy to do. It may also be a deliberate signal of amusement and and an invitation to laugh.

Smiling without opening the mouth, and particularly with lips firmly pressed together, may indicate embarrassment about unsightly teeth. It may also be a suppression of words ('I can see the funny side, but I'm not going to comment.').

A half-smile, on one side of the face, may indicate cynicism, sarcasm or uncertainty ('Sorry, I don't buy that idea.').

Smiling is also a sign of submission as the person effectively says 'I am nice and not a threat'.

Smiling in some cultures indicates a question or that you want the other person to speak.

Laughing

Beyond smiling, laughter shows greater pleasure and happiness. Whilst smiling may happen over a longer period, laughter is a relatively brief affair, happening for a few seconds.

There are many variants on laughter and we all laugh differently, from the suppressed titter to the loud and uproarious belly-laugh. Louder and less suppressed laughter may indicate someone who is less self-conscious. It may also be used by a person who is trying to gain attention.

In general, women laugh at men they like whilst men like women who laugh at them ('It's working! She likes me.'). This can lead to a satisfying bonding mechanism.

'Funny' often gets equated to 'nice' and 'harmless' and the use of humor thus can a way of sending friendship signals. Laughing at risqué jokes is a sign of acceptance of the other person (the alternative is to criticize or otherwise censure them).

Laughing and smiling at the misfortune of others is often socially unacceptable although we often find this funny (Germans call this 'schadenfreude'). In such cases you may see suppressed grins and giggles as the person tries desperately to hide their feeling of amusement. Laughs, for example may get disguised as coughs and the person may turn away to hide their expression.

Yawning

Yawning is opening the mouth wide and gulping in a large quantity of air. We do it when we are tired and blood oxygen is low.

Boredom can indicated by yawning, signalling that the other person is so uninteresting they are sending us to sleep, which makes it often impolite (also because it shows the inside of the body). This results often in the yawn being covered with the hand or concealed such as by turning the head or holding the mouth more closed than it actually want to be.

The gulping of air in yawning can also be in preparation for action and a stressed person may yawn more, or at least take some bigger breaths.

Sucking or biting

Sucking a finger is often an echo of doing this in childhood. Young children suck fingers or thumb as a breast substitute. This action is hence a comforter, done when the person is uncomfortable or stressed in some way. This can happen in general anxiety or specific situations such as when lying.

Variants on this include sucking or biting knuckles, the side of a hand or other parts of the body such as the lips or inner cheek. Sometimes a physical item is used as a substitute, such as a pen or pencil. Biting generally indicates greater stress than sucking.

TEETH BODY LANGUAGE

There's not a lot of body language with teeth, but this is a complete section, so here's details.

Biting

Teeth are made to bite, tear and grind. Exposing the teeth in a snarl is saying 'I am thinking of biting you' and is hence a primitive and potentially scary threat.

Actual biting is rare, but indicates the person has been reduced to a base position and is probably not thinking rationally.

Biting can also be affectionate, for example where lovers chew the other person's lip or ear. This can create arousal from the basic fear instinct but the person knows from the context that they are not in danger and hence reframes the arousal as pleasure. Gentle biting also stimulates nerve receptors and is thus similar to touch.

Biting the inside of the cheek or biting the lip can indicate suppression of a desire to speak. Lip biting or sucking can also be a comforting action when a person is anxious (perhaps as a substitute for thumb-sucking).

Young animals at play pretend to bite one another as they prepare for adulthood. When people play with friends they may also expose their teeth.

Smiling

Exposing the teeth in smiling tends to indicate extreme pleasure. People who are self-conscious and particularly if their teeth are not that attractive may try not to show their teeth when smiling.

Noise

Teeth can make a noise when banged or slid together. Chattering teeth may indicate extreme fear and is usually accompanied by shaking of the body. This may also indicate extreme coldness.

Grinding teeth can indicate suppressed anger or frustration as the person tensely tries not to speak.

Light tapping of the teeth can be mild frustration or thinking (it is similar in effect to tapping of a finger).

As with other repetitive action, teeth noise can also just be habit.

Tapping

Sometimes people tap their teeth with their nails, making a noise that echoes in the mouth. This can signal thinking or boredom. It may also be a deliberate interruption or irritant, although this is less likely.

TONGUE BODY LANGUAGE

The tongue is normally important in spoken body language. In practice it can also send some body language non-verbal signals.

Sticking out

A deliberate gesture of sticking out the tongue at a person is impolite, although considered rather childish and thus reflects as much on the person doing it. The gesture thus appears petulant unless it is done in an amusingly cheeky way. The rest of the face should indicate more of the intent. Cheeky tongue-poking is often followed by a smile or laughter.

Sticking out the tongue also can happen when the person is trying hard to do something. When this happens it traditionally appears at the side of the mouth.

When people are talking in romantic setting, sticking out the tongue can be a sign of lust.

Licking

The tongue can be used to lick. By oneself, pretty much the only thing the tongue can lick is the lips (although a more hidden way of this is licking the teeth).

Lip-licking may indicate desire, perhaps for another person and perhaps for food. Usually it is for what is in front of the licker.

Licking lips can also be an indicator of stress as the effects of tension reduce saliva flow and dry out the mouth.

As a deliberate signal to others it can be sexually enticing, saying 'I would like to like you'. As such, it can be very arousing, particularly when done slowly and with other flirting signals such as a slightly lowered head and steady gaze.

Licking another person can be extremely arousing and is typically done either as a part of foreplay or as a quick tease.

Biting it

Biting the tongue typically indicates that the biter wants to say something but somehow feels unable or unwilling to say what they want, perhaps for fear of offending or breaking social rules.

Inside the mouth

With mouth closed and tongue inside the mouth, you can still sometimes see what it is doing, although this is a hidden action and often the person themself does not realize they are doing this.

Pressed against the cheek it can indicate thinking and uncertainty. This can also indicate contempt and a form of duper's delight, especially when done briefly.

Pushed in front of the teeth, pushing out the lips, can also indicate uncertainty.

CHAPTER 7

Gesture, Stance, and Facial Expression

INTRODUCTION

Do we expect other cultures to adopt our customs or are we willing to adopt theirs? This might translate to how business or even foreign relations are to be conducted. Do we compromise or force others peoples to deal only on our terms? We may not have time to hear a language , but taking time to learn the "signals" is a powerful communicator.

As the global village continues to shrink and cultures collide, it is essential for all of us to become more sensitive, more aware, and more observant to the myriad motions, gestures, and body language that surround us each day. And as many of us cross over cultural borders, it would be fitting for us to respect, learn, and understand more about the effective, yet powerful "silent language" of gestures.

The world is a giddy montage of vivid gestures- traffic police, street vendors, expressway drivers, teachers, children on playground, athletes with their exuberant hugging, clenched fists and "high fives." People all over the world use their hands, heads, and bodies to communicate expressively. Without gestures, our world would be static and colorless. The social anthropologists Edward T. Hall claims 60 percent of all our communication is nonverbal. In that case, how can we possibly communicate with one another without gestures?

Gestures and body language communicate as effectively as words - maybe even more effectively. We use gestures daily, almost instinctively, from beckoning to a waiter, or punctuating a business presentation with visual signals to airport ground attendants guiding an airline pilot into the jetway or a parent using a whole dictionary of gestures to teach (or preach to) a child.

Gestures are woven inextricably in to our social lives, but also that the "vocabulary" of gestures, can be at once informative and entertaining... but also dangerous. Gestures can be menacing (two drivers on a freeway), warm (an open-armed welcome). instructive(a police man giving road directions, or even sensuous (the liquid movement of a Hawaiian hula dancer).

Bear in mind that the following gestures are in general use, but there may always be exceptions. In recent years, Western and contemporary values and ideas have become more popular and has either influenced, altered, and even replaced, some of the more traditional gestures, understanding human behavior is tricky stuff. No two people behave in precisely the same way. Nor do people from the same culture all perform exactly the same gestures and body language uniformly. For almost any gestures there will probably be a minority within a given nationality who might say "Well, some might attach that meaning to it, but to me it means..." and then they will provide a different interpretation.

In the world of gestures, the best single piece of advice is to remember the two A's - "Ask" and be "aware." If you see a motion or gesture that is new or confusing , ask a local person what it signifies. Then, be aware of the many body signs and customs around you.

THE ULTIMATE GESTURE

According to Roger G. Axtell, the "ultimate gesture" carries certain welcome characteristic unlike any other single gestures.

- First, this "ultimate gestures" is known everywhere- and I stress "everywhere"- in the world. It is absolutely universal.
- Second, it is rarely, if ever, misunderstood. Primitive tribes and world leaders alike know and use this gestures. The tribesmen - like you, no doubt - recognize it in others and use it themselves.
- Third, scientists believe this particular gesture actually releases chemicals called endorphins in to the system that create a feeling of mild euphoria.
- Fourth, as you travel around the world, this gesture may help you slip out of the prickliest of difficult situations.

What is this singular signal, this miracle mien, this giant of all gestures?

It is quite simply, the smile.

Use it freely, use it often.

BODY LANGUAGE COMPRISES GESTURE, STANCE, AND FACIAL EXPRESSION

These are all the more important when all eyes of an audience are upon you. When you are presenting, strong, positive body language becomes an essential tool in helping you build credibility, express your emotions, and connect with your listeners. It also helps your listeners focus more intently on you and what you're saying.

The tricky thing about body language is that you are usually unaware of the messages you're conveying nonverbally. When presenters see themselves on videotape, they're often surprised to see that their body language conveyed an entirely different message from the one they had intended. For example, some people actually shake their heads "no" when they say "yes."

Effective body language supports the message and projects a strong image of the presenter. Audiences respond best to presenters whose bodies are alive and energetic. Audiences appreciate movement when it is meaningful and supportive of the message.

The most effective movements are ones that reflect the presenter's personal investment in the message.

Anyone can utter a series of words; it is the presenter's personal connection to those words that can bring them to life for the audience. Presenters who care deeply about their material tend to use their entire bodies to support the message. Their gestures are large enough to embrace the room full of people. They stand tall and lean into the audience right from their feet, as if trying to shorten the distance between their message and the ears of the audience. Their faces express their passion while their eyes connect with the audience, focusing on one person at a time.

GESTURE

Do use your hands. They don't belong on your hips or in your pockets or folded across your chest either or held behind your back. Use them-to help emphasize a point, to express emotion, to release tension, and to engage your audience.

Most people have a gestural vocabulary at their disposal. Anyone can all think of a gesture that supports words such as "short" or "tall;" however, the gestures of everyday conversation tend to be too small and often too low to use in front of a large audience. Presenters need to scale their gestures to the size of the room. The most effective gestures arise from the shoulder, not the wrist or elbow. Shoulder gestures project better across the distance and release more of the presenter's energy, helping combat any tension that can build in the upper body (particularly under pressure).

Stance

How you stand in front of the room speaks before open your mouth. Your stance can tell the audience that you're happy, scared, confident, or uncomfortable. Audiences "read" these messages unthinkingly but unfailingly. Stance speaks. A balanced stance with weight even but slightly forward tends to say that the speaker is engaged with the audience. A slumped stance leaning to one side can says the speaker doesn't care.

The feet should point straight ahead, not quite shoulder-width apart. When not gesturing, the hands should sit quietly at the sides of the presenter. Letting the hands fall to the sides between gestures projects ease. These moments of stillness between gestures also have the effect of amplifying the gestures. Yes, you can move around, but remember to punctuate that movement with stillness. Constant motion, such as swaying, is a distraction that can annoy your listeners.

FACIAL EXPRESSION

The movements of your eyes, mouth, and facial muscles can build a connection with your audience. Alternatively, they can undermine your every word. Eye focus is the most important element in this process. No part of your facial expression is more important in communicating sincerity and credibility. Nothing else so directly connects you to your listeners-whether in a small gathering or a large group. Effective presenters engage one person at a time, focusing long enough to complete a natural phrase and watch it sink in for a moment. This level of focus can rivet the attention of a room by drawing the eyes of each member of the audience and creating natural pauses between phrases. The pauses not only boost attention, but also contribute significantly to comprehension and retention by allowing the listener time to process the message.

The other elements of facial expression can convey the feelings of the presenter, anything from passion for the subject, to depth of concern for the audience. Unfortunately, under the pressure of delivering a group presentation, many people lose their facial expression. Their faces solidify into a grim, stone statue, a thin straight line where the lips meet. Try to unfreeze your face right from the start. For example, when you greet the audience, smile! You won't want to smile throughout the entire presentation, but at least at the appropriate moments. It's only on rare occasions that you may need to be somber and serious throughout.

BRING IT ALL TOGETHER

While we all want to believe that it's enough to be natural in front of a room, it isn't really natural to stand up alone in front of a group of people. It's an odd and unusual thing that creates stress, tension, and stomach troubles. Being natural won't cut it. We need to be bigger, more expressive, and more powerful. It takes extra effort and energy. It also takes skill and practice. With so much depending on communication and communication depending on body language, it's worth getting it right. Work on your body language-gesture, stance, and facial expression-to make the most of every speaking opportunity.

CHAPTER 8

Customs and Etiquette

DIFFERENCES BETWEEN EASTERN AND WESTERN TRADITIONS

Nowadays, with the increasing contacts between people of different cultural backgrounds, cross-cultural communication becomes the world's growing trend. Etiquette vary in different regions, countries and social systems. Among different cultural traditions, there is a vast difference between the Eastern traditions and Western traditions. Eastern etiquette prevails in countries such as China, Japan, Korea, India and Singapore; while Western etiquette is practiced in countries such as the United States, England, Italy, Germany and France.

Characteristics of Eastern Traditions

1. focus on family love and kinship
2. modest and implicit
3. accept the reality and satisfy with current status
4. emphasize on common features (holistic)
5. reciprocity

Characteristics of Western Traditions

1. simple and practical (practicality)

2. advocate personal freedom
3. cherish time
4. free, equal and open-minded

WHAT IS ETIQUETTE?

The three fundamental elements that form etiquette include language (in writing or verbal form), behavior and costumes. The basic forms of etiquette vary depending on a number of factors such as living conditions, historical traditions, cultural mindset and ethnic customs. The variation of these factors resulted in the four common types of etiquette:

Protocol

It is the code of behavior in showing respect and friendship to each other in the course of interpersonal, social and international contacts.

Courtesy

It is he usual form in expressing greetings, regards, wishes and sympathy in daily life and sometimes in special socializing occasions. The expressions may vary from countries to countries due to regional and ethnic differences. Examples include nods and handshakes which are commonly accepted all over the world, or putting palms together in India (*Namaste*), or hugging and kissing in Europe and America.

Manner

It is the behavioral code in expressing modesty, respect and friendship among people by using words, facial expression and gestures. The forms of manners include:

1) appearance, grooming and deportment;
2) language and style of conversation;
3) apparel, clothing, hairstyle;

4) facial expression and gestures; and
5) ways in dealing with people, attitude, etc.

Ceremony

Those are the things that are said and done on a formal event or formal occasion. Examples include inspection of parade and cannon salutes when welcoming a head of foreign state or a head of government, curtain-unveiling, ribbon-cutting during exhibitions, or foundation laying for large projects.

ETIQUETTE AND THE HOSPITALITY INDUSTRY

During a visit, there are always interpersonal contacts including contacts between tourists, tourists between hopitality staff, and tourists/guests between local residents of the host country. These contacts are diversified in nature, we need "etiquette" to manage our behavior, enhance mutual understanding and friendship.

Hopitality /Tourism industry must provide tourists/guests with quality service etiquette in addition to the provision of tangible products and services such as transportation services, accommodation services and recreational facilities. Quality service etiquette aims to help tourism services staff to understand the different types of protocol, courtesy, manners and ceremony. Therefore, quality customer service etiquette is one of the essential factors for tourism industry in meeting the customers' demand for service satisfaction.

GREETING ETIQUETTE FOR MEETING PEOPLE FROM DIFFERENT COUNTRIES

Handshake

Handshake originated in Europe. It was meant to reassure each other that neither person held any weapons. Handshake is commonly accepted in most countries. Therefore, a decent handshake is a good way to show happiness when meeting a foreign guest. However, never use your left hand or both hands to shake hands with an

Indian because they never use their left hand except when using the washroom.

Bow

In some Asian countries such as South Korea (Republic of Korea) and Japan, people usually bow with their hands placing flat on their knees when they meet a friend. Bows are usually accompanied by verbal greetings. Graceful motion should be ensured when making a bow.

Hug

Before hugging, you should first have a certain understanding about the degree of friendship between both of you, and also the relevant customs. Otherwise, your hug could be turned down. In particular, when a gentleman meets a lady, he should observe if the lady has the intention to hug. It is advised that the gentleman should wait for the lady to hint for a hug first.

Cheek Kissing

Cheek kissing is prevailing in many countries. Generally, only the right side of the cheek would be kissed. This etiquette is especially popular in countries such as Spain and Italy.

In addition, there are other forms of greeting etiquettes. For example, salute is an etiquette generally practiced by soldiers; putting palms together (*Namaste*) is a religious etiquette; hand kissing is an etiquette practiced in the upper class in Europe and the US.

When a gentleman meets a noble lady and the lady holds out her hand with her palm facing downward, the gentleman should take the offered hand and touch it with his lips. Hand kissing will not be performed unless the lady holds out her hand.

We should determine the form of etiquette depending on the country, religion and personal background of the person receiving the greetings. Otherwise, we may probably offend other people. Certainly, it would be safer if you express pleasant facial expressions first and observe the intention of the other party before determining which form of etiquette would be appropriate.

ETIQUETTE AND TABOOS

The differences of cultural traditions and values vary in accordance to the differences between countries, regions, nationalities and economic development. In addition, tourists are different in terms of employments, genders, ages and lifestyles, which in turn have differences in their consumption patterns. In order to provide tourists with satisfactory services, tourism staff should have a good understanding of these differences.

For example, Westerners treat the number "13" as ominous. Japanese also avoid the number "13", but their reason is not due to the number itself, instead it is related to the sum of "1" and "3", which makes "4". In Japanese, the pronunciation of "4" is similar to that of "death". If a service staff presents 4 pieces of gifts to a Japanese customer, it would be regarded as a curse. Some nationalities have taboos about colors. For example, black is the color used in funerals in Europe and the US; blue is unlucky in the eyes of Belgians; in Brazil purple is sadness. Therefore, it is important to observe the customs and taboos of a region before going abroad.

Asia

The complexions of Asian people are more or less similar, but their etiquette and taboos in the aspects of politics, religion and customs may be different. It is necessary to know them before travelling. When travelling to Buddhist countries such as Sri Lanka, you may chat with monks freely in the street, but you must be respectful. For example, you have to bend a bit and lower your head when speaking to them. There is no exception even if you were the president of that country.

In India, never jostle about if you see a cow ahead. Any disrespectful acts before a cow would irritate Indians because cows are considered sacred in Hinduism. As a common practice in the Southeast Asian region and India, passing things to others with the left hand means disrespect and malice. These are things that tourists should keep in mind.

Middle East

The Middle East is a vast region made up of a variety of countries. Some countries such as Lebanon is one of the most Europeanized countries in the Middle East, but some Islamic countries such as Saudi Arabia is quite conservative. In terms of tourism, the Middle East is not a very popular tourist area due to complicated political issues. Nevertheless, Middle East countries always present a mysterious ambience that attracts people.

When traveling to these countries, tourists should pay extra attention to the local religions. For example, in Saudi Arabia, women would cover their entire body except their eyes. The Jewish Sabbath begins from sunset on Friday to sunset of the next day every week. During this period, all government offices, banks and offices in Jerusalem would be closed. In Afghanistan, when people greet each other, they shake hands or hug each other twice. Tourists should never wear clothes with star patterns when travelling in the Middle East. It is because star is the symbol of the Israeli flag. It will easily offend local people.

Africa

Africans have a strong sense about tribes. People in African countries take the concept of nation lightly. Therefore, before communicating with African people, it is important to know what tribe they belong. Tourists should pay attention to appellations when communicating with people in Africa. For example, black people in Africa do not mind being called "Black", but never call them "Negro" because this term denotes racial discrimination. In addition, it is a taboo to discuss skin color in Africa. Black Africans distinguish themselves from African Americans very clearly. They believe that black people in the United States are different from themselves as those were slaves trafficked from Africa. When travelling in Africa, shake hands firmly and sincerely with local people because they would judge your sincerity by the firmness of handshake. When travelling in Africa, you need to keep in mind that many local people believe that taking a photo of someone would draw away the "spirit" of the person being photographed. In their eyes, cameras are similar to guns. As a result, it is an improper and unforgivable action to take photos of them. If you want to take a photo of the local people when you are traveling in Africa, you must first ask for their permission.

Europe

The principle of "Lady first" is stressed in European etiquette. "Sorry" and "Thank you" are the most frequently used expressions in interpersonal communication and socialized occasions. There are certain table manners to observe in European style dining. For example, toothpicks are generally not provided on tables. If you bring your own toothpicks, do not use them in front of others. It is better to use them in the washroom if you really need to. Never pickup the plates to eat, however, silverware and glassware are allowed. Europeans seldom drink water during meals, and they are usually served with alcoholic drinks. People who do not want alcoholic drinks are usually served with juices.

In Europe, say "Excuse me" when you pass by others at a narrow space. But instead of jostling, you should turn your body to face those who are seated and move along slowly. Similar to the Americans, Europeans address people by names directly once they know each other. It is impolite to address others by "You".

America

Americans and Canadians are outgoing and friendly. They welcome foreign guests. It is considered rude by Americans and Canadians if someone wears pajamas or slippers in meeting with other people. Venezuelans hate peacocks because they believe peacocks are ominous. As a result, no patterns of peacocks or ornaments made of peacock feathers are welcome. In Chile, it should be noted that local people there would take four meals a day: breakfast, lunch (around 1:00p.m.), tea (around 4:00p.m.) and supper (around 9:00p.m.). When attending social functions in Chile, one should arrive 15-30 minutes after the invitation time. Argentineans are picky about clothes. A man usually has to wear a vest if the suit he wears is single-breasted. Pay attention to the color of clothes when travelling in Mexico. Mexicans consider purple as the colour of a coffin. Therefore, when offering a gift to Mexicans, do not wrap it with purple wrapping paper.

BODY LANGUAGE AND BUSINESS ETIQUETTE

Body language can make or break a deal. How you carry yourself when engaged in conversation is often as important as what you say. Body language is nonverbal, but it communicates volumes about you nonetheless.

With almost infinite symbolic interpretations for body language, no wonder people are nervous about it! Your best bet is to know about some of the body-language pits you can fall into and how to avoid them.

Standing

When you stand, keep your back straight, middle section in alignment with your back, shoulders back, and head up. This posture connotes comfort with yourself and ease in the situation.

Slouching, sticking your belly out, stuffing your hands in your pockets, and folding your arms defensively all suggest aggressive unease.

Sitting

Take care in the way you sit, for no other position connotes so much on its own. Think of the diversity of sitting positions that you've seen in business meetings, from practically horizontal to alert and upright. Sit with a straight back and with your legs together in front of you or crossed, either at the knee or at the ankle. Normally, women don't cross their legs, but men are allowed. Avoid jiggling your knee, which is a sign of nervousness (and can be pretty annoying to people sitting near you).

Hands

Some people talk with their hands; others stand with their hands glued to their sides. Most people haven't the foggiest notion what their hands are doing when they talk.

Using your hands can be effective sometimes, aggressive sometimes, and irrelevant most of the time. Controlling your hands takes effort and willpower. Monitor your hand movements. Avoid making sweeping, cappuccino-clearing gestures during meetings. If you have to, sit on your hands.

Head Movements

Head movements communicate important information. Nodding in agreement can be immensely helpful to others, but too much nodding makes you look like a bobble-head doll. Shaking your head can signal disagreement or disapproval, but avoid shaking your head too much.

Facial Expressions

Facial expressions are crucial in your repertoire of body language. No other part of your body can convey the immense richness of nonverbal communication that your face does. For example:

- Smiles are important signals of generosity and nonaggression. But forced smiles signal that you can barely tolerate the other person.

- Likewise, frowns signal disagreement, disapproval, and sometimes anger. But they can also suggest hard thinking and focused concentration.

These facial expressions are the most obvious ones, but hundreds of others exist: an arched eyebrow, flared nostrils, a bitten lip, a grimace . . . and on and on. Every one of them has a culturally agreed-on set of meanings.

Take a day to monitor your most frequently used facial expressions and assess their appropriateness and their effectiveness. You'll probably be surprised by the types of messages your expressions transmit!

Eyes

Maintain eye contact when talking with others. Do not study your hands or clean your fingernails while others are talking. When talking in a group, make eye contact with everyone; don't focus on only one person.

CHAPTER 9

Hospitality Staff Taught to Read Body Language to Improve Customer Service Skills

"Training is the process that provides employees with the knowledge and the skills required to operate within the systems and standards set by management." (*Sommerville*)

"Training, in the most simplistic definition, is an activity that changes people's behavior." (*McCleland*)

STAFF TRAINING IN HOSPITALITY INDUSTRY

In modern hospitality business, it is all about competence in people, and especially the employees qualities. The level of service quality depends on the qualities of employees. The qualities are about knowledge, skills and thoughts which lead to a hospitality s survival and development. Therefore, staff training is essential in many ways; it increases productivity while employees are armed with professional knowledge, experienced skills and valid thoughts; staff training also motivates and inspires workers by providing employees all needed information in work as well as help them to recognize how important their jobs are.

Training and development can be seen as a key instrument in the implementation of HRM practices and policies. Successful hotels always include staff training as their important development strategy.

THE IMPORTANCE OF STAFF TRAINING

Staff training is a significant part as well as the key function of Human Resource Management and Development; it is the crucial path of motivating employees and increasing productivity in the business.

With the development of the technologies and the whole business environment, employees are requested to be more skilled and qualified, even if you are a good employee today, you could be out of the line some other day if you do not keep studying. A company needs organized staff training if wants to be competitive among others.

Staff training is the key task to help everyone in the company to be more united. An enterprise could hire experienced employees or train employees to be skilled. When the company trains their own staff, by providing and forming a harmonious atmosphere, accurate work specification and the passion of work, team spirit will be built between employees and management team within the process.

Training of work tasks is one of the main aspects of staff training, including principles at work, professional knowledge and skills, by offering employees these essentials, staff training helps personal abilities match with business requirements.

Training could be enormously demanding and should be in-depth; lack of training or poor training brings out high employee turnover and the delivery of substandard products and services.

BENEFITS OF STAFF TRAINING

Staff training enhances the capabilities of employees and strengthens their competitive advantage. Effective training will improve the personal characters and professional abilities. Not only employees, management and organization would benefit from staff training, customers and guests benefit as well, because of the received quality products and services.

BENEFITS THE EMPLOYEE

Increases job satisfaction and recognition

During the training, employees will be introduced what is the work is about, how to do, what kind of role does the job play in the whole business, it helps them to understand their work better and also love what they do by understanding the work.

Encourages self-development and self-confidence

After systemized training, employees will understand what important role their jobs play, and with the information, knowledge and experiences obtained during the training, they will be more confident with their work, so that better services will be provided.

Moves employee closer to personal goals

Employees gained not only professional knowledge and skills during training, training also broads their choices on setting career targets. They can get the opportunity to get to know other positions, increases the possibilities of promotions in the meantime.

Helps the employee become an effective problem solver

Practical experience can be taught and guided in the training; employees will learn the methods of solving problem or complaints during training.

Allows the employee to become productive more quickly

By training, employees get familiar with their work tasks, advanced knowledge and techniques which improve their capabilities, increases productivity.

BENEFITS THE MANAGEMENT

Aids in evaluating employee performance

People who are responsible for training will find out those employees during training, who are quick learners, who have better knowledge and skills, so that different methods of training can be chosen, therefore, better results will be acquired.

Aids in sustaining systems and standards

Within the training, employees will be introduced to the principles and standards of the hospitality, together with the policies and procedures; hence hospitality can sustain its standards and system with the help of training.

Helps identify employees for promotions or transfers

During the training, employees abilities and personalities will be easily identified by experienced trainers, or some employees are more suitable for other positions, hotels can adjust and make best use of employees knowledge and abilities.

BENEFITS THE ORGANIZATION

Leads to improved profitability

Owing to the growth of productivity and better services after training, it is more promised for the hospitality to have more profits in return.

Reduces accidents and safety violations

Without organized training and guidance, especially employees who work with dangerous facilities, accidents are easily occurred, training can help organizations to prevent accidents.

Aids in organizational development

Hotels need to develop their technologies and way of working in order to be competitive, and staff training assures the competitiveness, because training will bring good quality, effectiveness and loyal customers to the hotels.

Reduces wastage and costly employee turnover

Wastage and damages in different departments are commonly found out in hospitality operation, with the help of staff training; unnecessary wastage and damages can be avoided. Regular trainings can decrease work pressures and employee turnover, as a result, less labor cost will be spent and better service can be achieved.

A need of training always results from the difference between an ideal expect for employees performances and the actual performances. Trainings can also be provided for new employees to help them get familiar with the work environment and tasks etc. HR department should consider the related aspects for example job analysis, performance objectives etc.

The second step in the training cycle is the planning of the training. Planning is separated into specifying training objectives, designing training program, selecting training methods. Training goals, training method, duration, program structure, location and selection of trainees etc. practical problems are to be answered in the planning stage.

After successfully planning the training, then the training program should be effectively carried out following the plan. The trainer should be well prepared and skillful, and the trainees should be actively participating in the training.

Evaluation of the training is an unavoidable stage in the training process, to get the feedback helps adjusting and organizing future trainings. Plans for future training can be done in this stage. Evaluation is the ending stage of a training cycle but at the same time it is the basis for the new training cycle.

STAFF TRAINING IN INTERNATIONAL PERSPECTIVE

As hospitality business is often on an international level, so that Staff training should also be internationalized. Cross-culture training needed to be taken into consideration when planning and designing trainings. Language training became especially important in international staff training.

Staff Training in International HRM (IHRM) is through various methods, attending courses and lectures in different schools or training centers, by using materials like readings, recordings, movies etc. to assist trainings. Since culture is a key factor in IHRM, therefore, culture topic is treated more seriously and carefully, employees should be trained well to deal with possible cultural misunderstandings or even conflicts. Practical information should be provided during the training, role play, simulations, and meetings with foreign employees will help the trainees to understand better.

HOW TO TRAIN YOUR HOSPITALITY STAFF TO ATTEND TO GUESTS?

Every member of the team at a hospitality has to learn customer service skills that go above and beyond a guest's expectations. While some employees may come to the company with amazing people skills and years of customer service under their belt, it is important to train all employees to get everyone on the same page.

You want to deliver a consistent experience to all of your guests whether they are ordering dinner to the room, interacting with housekeeping or checking out at the front desk. Having a formalized way of interacting with guests, conducting standard processes and providing superior service will help make the expectations clear.

Having this formalized way of interacting with guests will help the property run smoothly, but it requires some effort on the front

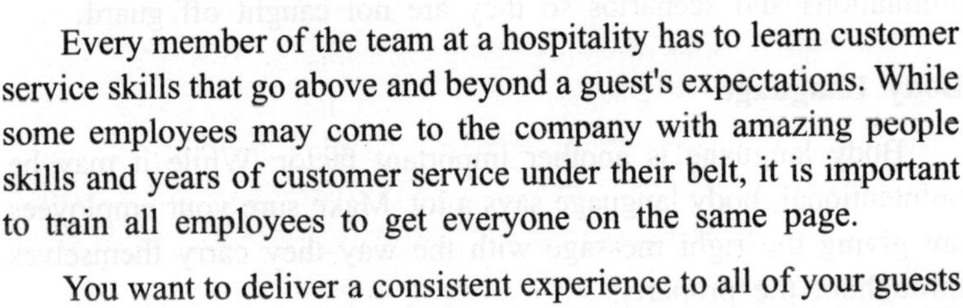

end. Management needs to train new employees to attend to guests and give intermittent refresher courses to current employees. While it is important to keep key traits in mind while hiring new employees, many skills can be learned.

Ensure your property is putting its best face forward and focus on these aspects when training the hospitality staff to attend to guests:

Communication

Communication is possibly the most important part of customer service. The way in which your employees interact with guests can make or break an experience. Employees need to be cool, calm and collected, but they also need to be accommodating and supportive as well. They need to be thoroughly trained with interactive simulations and scenarios so they are not caught off guard.

Body Language

Body language is another important factor. While it may be unintentional, body language says a lot. Make sure your employees are giving the right message with the way they carry themselves throughout the property.

Department Expectations

There should be a clear understanding of what is expected from each role. While team members can go above and beyond their call of duty, a task or job should always be assigned to a specific role. Each employee should know which duties are assigned to each department. While it is important to know what is expected of each employee, it is also useful so employees will know where to direct specific questions. With clear expectations, guests will enjoy better service and more organized interaction with staff.

Training and Development

Training is the most crucial aspect as it puts your staff in a better position to contribute to the hotel's success. Make training a part of day-to-day management, so it's not considered as an additional task. This goes for both staff and management.

Behavioir

Train your staff on their behavior management. You need to teach them how to identify customers' needs and requests, and how to conduct themselves when assisting the customer.

You have to encourage your staff to take a guest journey and see everything from a guest's point of view as often as possible. This will help them put the whole customer experience into perspective.

Motivating Your Hospitality Staff To Perform Better

A recent study pointed out that the hospitality industry exhibits high turnover rates, as high as 95% for certain hospitality properties. This high turnover rate costs the hospitality industry several billion dollars per year, globally. The hospitality staff that fuels this industry is constantly expected to deliver impeccable services while being polite and welcoming. Truth is - being a part of the hospitality industry is not a cakewalk and it can make anybody a little hot under their collars compared to other jobs.

How to Motivate Hospitality Staff?

Retaining a loyal hospitality staff involves an investment of motivation, dedication and devotion of the hospitality management higher-ups. The blue print of the hospitality management should involve a firm agenda that motivates the existing employees as well as prepares them to face the challenges in their day-to-day tasks.

Set Growth Parameters

When hiring for a specific position in the hospitality staff, it motivates the individual to know and assess his/her growth curve in the organization. The reminder of incentives and intermittent bonuses can buoy anybody's job perspective.

Offer Competitive Growth

Set growth targets and dole out incentives to the staff who outshine the rest to achieve the goal. Healthy competition pays well for any industry; prizes are like tiny baits. The need to rally, to build growth in the hospitality business can motivate your staff to earn more bonuses.

Prepare them for the Challenge

In case your hospitality staff feels like a lamb on a sacrificial pyre, it is not going to help in achieving employee support. Hospitality employees should be trained to handle the events and pressures of their day-to-day tasks. Given that the hospitality industry works on person to person interaction, it is demanding for any person to continue to be polite, courteous and well-mannered at all points of the job. Conduct regular counselling sessions, training camps and casual meetings to gauge and motivate your hospitality staff.

Remember that it is Human Science and not Rocket Science

Hospitality industry is primed as the one of the best-polished professions, wherein presentability and approachability can go a long way to earn goodwill, appreciation and loyalty. Given that this profession delves on person to person interaction, it can heavily involve investment of emotions and physicality of your hospitality staff. Keeping your hospitality staff polished, congenial and brimming is the biggest factor to bring out the best in them. Give your hospitality staff ample time to interact and develop a sense of belonging and significant role-play in the organization.

There is no better motivator than knowing how much you are valued in an organization. Giving your hospitality staff the impetus to perform better, and gaining their trust and loyalty is a pivotal part of your hospitality management. As the management, you can ease their day-to-day tasks by implementing certain property management tools and recommending the best practices in the industry. From the front desk operations to the housekeeping department, hospitality staff should feel motivated to be on their toes 24/7 and still maintain a smile on their face. Make sure your hospitality work policies give your employees both growth, success and fulfilment in their jobs.

CHAPTER 10

'Luxury Touch' Delivering in the Hospitality Industry

Truly luxury hotels have the ability to engage their guests in a distinctive, exclusive and meaningful way not found elsewhere. They create a certain mystique that becomes almost addictive, bringing guests back time and time again. The hotel is an architectural gem and a landmark; and the epitome of luxury.

We live and breathe a distinct luxury style that is embedded in our hotel's culture. In order to offer the 'best of the best' to our young-minded sophisticated guests of any age, we empower our staff to consistently deliver on luxury service expectations in bold and unique ways that ultimately differentiate our brand from other hotel experiences. With luxury rooms and suites offering world-class panoramic ocean views, guests can indulge in a long-term leisure or business stay, or enjoy a romantic escape while watching the sunset or moonrise over the Pacific.

Today, the concept of luxury is not just about extravagant hotel features, which are plentiful here. Highlights of our distinctive luxury touches include 24-hour concierge service by an international staff, lush courtyard with elevated pool and cabanas, first-class epicurean restaurant, Suite 700 - our posh 360 degree view rooftop bar and lounge, suites with ocean views, lightning speed wireless Internet access, around-the-clock in-room dining, indulgent bath products, and the plushest robes by Frette. Everything is carefully curated to provide a comfortable and exuberant, yet deeply inspiring and exhilarating, getaway. People do not forget how you make them feel.

Luxury is about the convergence of a wide array of luxury offerings, a connection with engaging service staff and opportunities for unique cultural experiences that form a truly memorable and indulgent experience for a lush life. Rather than aspiring to luxury, today's guests want to be inspired by luxury touches throughout their stay.

There is no standard definition of luxury because luxury is a matter of personal interpretation. It represents different things to different people and is formed by an individual understanding of what is and is not considered luxurious. Most people agree that luxury is an indulgence, beyond the ordinary and exceeds expectations in a surprising manner. Luxury tends to evoke feelings of being special; it raises expectations and allows people to live without pre- defined limits. From a sense of style and comfort, a legendary location, pampered attention, extravagance or ultra-simplicity, luxury is many things to many people. But one thing is clear - luxury delivers unexpected pleasures that exceed expectations in original ways.

THE HOTEL SHANGRI-LA CULTURE

The culture of the Hotel Shangri-la brand flows from a global vision from our hotel's owner, and propagates to every aspect of the hotel's design, atmosphere and service. It relies heavily on Tamie's personal taste and astute sense of aesthetics. A strong and visionary leader, her goal is for Hotel Shangri-la's exhilarating and elevating personality-driven brand to inform every aspect of the guest experience and vividly communicate, and share with them, her unique and particular point of view.

Guests can't help but notice the exquisite appointments that represent both the Art Moderne and earlier Art Deco periods. Among these touches is a 1939 cobalt blue Chase Martini Set reflecting the tone for this post-depression era, full of hope and lavish, swanky social gatherings. An original Erté adorns the wall of one of the suites. Authentic American pottery from such makers as Roseville and Weller graces shelves. Punctuating the moderne lines of suites are a statuette by Frankart, a centerpiece by Kensington, and compotes by Farber Brothers with ruby red, amber, and cobalt blue glass, characteristic hues of the day.

The aesthetic, opulence and simplicity combined with the hotel's architectural elements help create our property's distinct culture. We also have a number of key concepts and core service philosophies that guide the way we operate. A welcome and inclusive environment infuses our staff with corporate pride and leverages our culture for the enjoyment of our guests.

Guests want to feel good when they stay at a luxury hotel, and they also want to relax. They desire a sense of escape, but they also crave vibrancy. At the Hotel Shangri-la, our brand perfectly reconciles these juxtaposed elements. Style, design, comfort, intimacy and location are just a few of the reasons visitors choose to stay at Hotel Shangri-la.

EXPERIENTIAL OFFERINGS

We differentiate our luxury boutique property by being a uniquely authentic and experiential hotel - we are anything but ordinary.

The atmosphere and ambiance creates an experiential culture and the hotel continues to be a popular hideaway for a wide variety of guests from presidents and celebrities to artists, tastemakers, insiders and world travelers, and everyone in between who wants to be indulged. It is encoded into the DNA of our brand to be spontaneous, flexible and responsive when we see an opportunity to enhance any aspect of a guest's experience.

Owner Tamie Adaya is a renowned social architect with a passion for bringing together creative people from film, fashion, art, jewelry, music, design and literature to orchestrate inspiring social exchanges.

She regularly does this via her popular invite-only salons held in the Shangri-la Dining Room with an intimate group of exciting, dynamic and influential people from diverse backgrounds - gathering for fun or learning. Recently, she hosted a series of art and fashion events during BritWeek with exciting talent such as British fashion designer, milliner and corset-maker Mich Dulce, for a poolside jubilee swing-dance party; artist Matthew Stone, named most influential person in the arts in the UK under 30 by the Sunday Times for a Salon; and world renowned artist KESH, who unveiled her KESH 4 Shangri-la custom art pieces designed exclusively for the hotel to the public for the first time.

Being a nexus of culture has earned the hotel its distinctive reputation as the word-of-mouth watering hole for the cognoscenti, bringing social style, luxury, spontaneity and refined experiences to share with all our guests.

BACK TO BASICS

While luxury hotel service continues to evolve, our core philosophy encompasses delivering VIP guest experiences that are pleasant, relaxed and comfortable. Instead of an over-reliance on technology, we subscribe to personalized and individualized service and pay attention to every little detail. From the minute we greet our guests with a smile, to the time we say farewell until the next time, we demonstrate that our passion for being of service is foremost in all our customer interactions.

Getting to know our guests on an emotional level and offering them small gestures to show we care creates a special connection. This is our one-on-one, in-person delivery of luxury touches that happens because of the internal alignment of our goals and expectations, and the dedication of our hotel staff. While we embrace technology for the convenience and comfort of our guests, we prefer to offer guests ultra-personalized service which we have mastered to perfection.

By placing additional emphasis on knowing more about our guests, we are able to indulge them in luxury brand experiences that are highly personalized and appropriately customized for each of their visits.

ORGANIC SERVICE

Personalized luxury is what our guests experience when staying with us. It's instinctively based, anticipatory in nature and delivers the preferred level of attention depending on each guest's needs at that moment. Tamie coined the term 'organic service,' which is an essential element of our guest experience because hotel staff uses their innate, finely-tuned people skills to determine exactly what kind of service a guest requires.

A jet-lagged guest checking in might want to be shown to their room as quickly as possible with minimal interaction, whereas a family breakfasting poolside planning a day trip might appreciate attentiveness, informal conversation and perhaps some recommendations on local sightseeing.

Anticipating the unexpressed wishes of our guests allow us to provide for each guest's needs in real-time - recognizing who wants service and who desires privacy - so each guest's needs are met according to their personal preference. An offer to deliver a pot of coffee for a guest departing very early is just the type of unexpected, yet appreciated anticipatory service our hotel is known for.

LUXURY DIFFERENTIATORS

Luxury touches are in the small details, and we take this very seriously. No matter how small a gesture, it can make a big difference in a guest's overall experience with us. From offering a birthday greeting, bringing a favorite cocktail or delivering a fresh fruit basket to the suite, taking time to identify and provide surprising luxury elements for our guests on a consistent basis differentiates our style of service.

A deep sense of luxury is also expressed in the ambiance of the hotel - the stunning décor in the lobby, fresh flowers in the dining room, and the lush green Courtyard where guests can be pampered in one of the fully-outfitted private cabanas. An onsite indoor fitness room is nearby and steps away is the Sybaris Rejuvenation Lounge where guests can enjoy holistic treatments from the ancient Tibetan Ku Nye Body Treatment to Reflexology, Reiki and a variety of luxury massages and body rejuvenation sessions.

Our philosophy is simple. We go to great lengths to ensure our style of service is intimate and cordial, providing all the comforts needed for guests to enjoy their stays. At the same time, we exercise discretion to allow guests privacy. Because we have so many international guests - during a three month period recently we welcomed guests from 21 countries -- we also offer a global ambassador service through our knowledgeable concierges and our staff who speak over twelve languages.

Guests are always greeted by friendly and helpful staff that smile frequently, say hello and ask if they can help, which makes people feel appreciated, valued and happy.

With our high staff-to-guest ratio, the ability to go above and beyond for our guests becomes the norm. For example in our dining room, the chef may prepare a special dish not on the menu for our returning guests or bring them a 'compliments of the chef' appetizer in advance of the main course as an unexpected special gesture.

First Impressions at Touch Points

Our corporate philosophy is to ensure that each guest experiences luxury service at all touch points, because that is what creates those critical first impressions. Here are a few highlights of how we differentiate our service:

- Reservations
- Hotel reservations can be made through the common channels based on guest preference and convenience.
- Special requests are graciously accommodated and they can made at the time of the reservation - whether for bedding

preference, any special food items or special treatment of our linen and towels. All guests have to do is ask.

- Check-in
  - We pre-register our guests whenever possible and upon their arrival at the valet, they are personally escorted straight to their suite where we finish the check-in process.
  - Seasonally, we offer a special complimentary drink at the check in desk while our guest completes the formalities.
- Dining room / Suite 700
  - When it comes to our food and beverage service, the luxury touch opportunities are unlimited and range from special food items based on a guest's preferences to having the chef prepare a guest's own "catch of the day" according to their taste.
- Departure formalities
  - We believe our departing guests deserve the same level of attention as when they arrive, so we can further strengthen that emotional connection with them. We end every guest experience with a fond farewell, warm goodbye and a sincere invitation to return.
  - Addressing guests by their names whenever possible, we strive to make people feel special. In addition, we may place a bottle of water in a guest's car upon departure, assist them with packing their luggage or arrange special airport handling to expedite flight check-in, security clearance and departure.

DELIVERING ON THE LUXURY PROMISE

If you ask one of our employees to point the way to Suite 700, The Dining Room or the fitness center, chances are you will receive a personal escort to where you want to go. Our staff is taught to own the guest relationship and is empowered to make sure each

person's experience is enjoyable and memorable. At the Hotel Shangri-la, it's everyone's job to take care of our guests.

EXCEPTIONAL STAFFING

Our ability to attract great staff stems from the fact that we understand and adhere to exceptional international service standards. We seek personnel who are organic learners - individuals with a natural curiosity from within - who have the ability to understand and interpret the influences around them. Organic learning is exciting and invigorating, and tends to be contagious among our staff.

We also look for people who possess the right mix of personality characteristics to be able to attentively and professionally serve our sophisticated guests. They demonstrate sincerity, a positive attitude, tenacity, autonomy to solve customer requests, a passionate desire to be helpful and endless patience for handling each guest's needs. Our staff knows that timing is critical when facing a problem and the faster an issue is resolved to the complete satisfaction of the guest, the better the outcome of the experience.

In addition to the key personality traits, another important quality for our staff is the ability to provide a calming and confident presence when guests are faced with stressful situations. The skill to stay calm, address the issue quickly and compassionately, and offer an unexpected finishing touch makes all the difference in the world to our guests. We have mastered the art of the apology when things do not meet expectations or we make a mistake. Always handled in an individual and sensitive manner, our guest communications are designed to not only resolve the problem but strengthen our future guest relations.

EMPLOYEE RECOGNITION AND REWARDS

Research shows there is a positive linkage between employee performance and employee engagement and recognition. We understand the importance of this correlation and have implemented a hotel-wide employee recognition program for the staff. Some basics that should be considered include:

1. **Understand the situation** - In selecting an employee to recognize, we weigh all aspects of performance, including financial performance, guest metrics and other types of feedback to select our employee of the month. Given that our team has all the tools available to exceed our guests' expectations, we seek to identify employees that consistently go above and beyond in their customer service actions. In some cases, we choose a staff member who may not have access to the tools, yet still exceeds expectations.
2. **Consider the culture** - Feedback is a critical aspect of any employee recognition program and our goal is to bring balance to the process. We know that some staff docs not have the natural feedback opportunities that others have. However, they are also a critical part of the overall operational success. Our team of international staff comes from various backgrounds - some are born leaders - others followers. We

identify those who are creative and willing to think outside the box, because this not only helps achieve our corporate goals, but energizes and motivates our entire team.

3. **Management support** - Our executive and management team is involved in the selection and recognition presentation for all employees so we can demonstrate that their efforts are a major contributing factor to our operation's success.
4. **Understand the overall value of the program** - In addition, management also shares some of the highlights of the employee's exceptional performance during the presentation to clearly focus not only the value of the program, but the critical role that each staff member makes.
5. **Importance of short-term and achievable goals** - A program that does not focus on achievable goals will not succeed. We look for attainable accomplishments, progress from previous months and recognize employees regularly for achieving their goals.
6. **Promote and publicize** - We feel strongly that sharing employee recognition awards through various channels, including our internal and guest newsletters, fosters our inclusive and respectful culture. This way, other staff knows who is receiving recognition, and more importantly, they understand why they are being recognized as role models.

COMPETITIVE ADVANTAGES

Our strategies are rooted in an intense understanding of our guest segments, including the dynamics of the current marketplace and focus on our social media platform. We are striving to go back to basics with our service culture and provide an organic "home away from home" that allows our guests to be inspired by their surroundings, complemented with "personalized and customized" service.

We like to consider the executive management team as our "lifestyle" team that will accommodate a guest's needs from personal

shopping; scheduling an after-hours visit to an Art Gallery; hosting events in various unique locations throughout the City, such as special jewelry stores for a private viewing; or even chartering a private jet for a day trip. To satisfy the needs of our special guests, we continually push the envelope to deliver the best of the best with a "lifestyle" smile.

MEASUREMENT AND BENCHMARKING

Naturally, to track progress we have to be able to measure our success and this is where measurement and benchmarking plays a key role. We do this through many of the common guest feedback tools, including Trip Advisor and other review/rating forums. Our benchmarking goals are established for our team and all feedback obtained is shared with the entire group. We believe every employee has an equal stake in meeting our goals, as well as solving any service recovery issues. We have to learn and take action and measure not just the numbers, but the emotional connections we make with our guests.

CONCLUSION

Every member in the organization is a brand ambassador when it comes to serving our guests. Whether it is front-line staff or those behind-the-scenes, consistently delivering a luxury touch to all of our guests is of paramount importance. As management, we understand how best to manage guest expectations and luxury experiences, service standards, employee training and coaching, plus dealing with service gaps and take decisive actions to deliver on the luxury promise. This allows us to provide a distinctively more memorable experience that keeps our guests returning year after year.

CHAPTER 11

Body Language and Professionalism

INCREASE YOUR TIPS: BODY LANGUAGE AND PROFESSIONALISM WILL EARN YOU MORE THAN PRAISE

As a server or bartender, you're often the first, and last, staff member a customer encounters. Your interactions will set the tone for the evening so you want to greet your customers warmly, and leave them reflecting on a positive experience once they head for the door. You only get one chance to make a first impression, so make sure it's a solid one. Professionalism and competence are very important, but so is projecting a great attitude and body language.

It's important to remember that good food, drinks and a great ambiance are not the only components to a great night out. Have you ever had poor service or a standoffish server? Experiences like this can play huge into your overall impression of an establishment. On the flipside, a positive attitude and a smile can go a long way toward making patrons feel relaxed and welcome. Not only will you put your guests into a good frame of mind, projecting a positive attitude and body language will help you to relax and enjoy your job as well. And, as an added bonus, positive body language and professionalism set the tone for an enjoyable evening and can net you greater tips. Here are a few easy body language dos and don'ts for hospitality workers:

1. **Smile**. A smile is the first social cue your guests will pick up on, and can immediately set the tone for a positive interaction. A genuine smile conveys friendliness and a can-do attitude.
2. **Don't cross your arms or slouch**. Crossing your arms over your chest tells your customer that you're bored, bothered or closed to them. The same thing goes for hosts and other hospitality staff, slouching over the host stand with your arms crossed is NOT the first sight your customers should see when they walk in the door; you're showing them that you're not having a good time and would rather be someplace else. Stand up straight and make a great impression.
3. **Pay attention and remain engaged**. When taking a guest's order, make sure you're turned to face them and pay attention. Restaurants and bars can be loud and busy at times, but don't get distracted and turn your gaze elsewhere. A guest wants to feel like they have your attention and an interested expression or nod to confirm you've heard their order is all it takes.

Sometimes it's the little things that make the biggest difference. What tips would you give someone to improve on their body language?

Here are some of Eaton's techniques for topping up your tips:

- **Be professional, clean** (especially your hands!), and positive in your approach.Being positive, though, doesn't mean becoming the diner's new best friend. According to Eaton, many people find the "Hi, I'm Kristin, and I'll be your server tonight" approach off-putting and vaguely uncomfortable. "You don't want a friend; it's a business transaction," he says.
- **Consider your body language**. If you're not carrying something to the table, your hands should be in front or behind so you appear engaged in what you're doing. Hands in your pockets or at your side indicate a lack of interest.

- **Don't touch the customer**. Again, Eaton feels this is too personal and can make diners feel uneasy.
- **Be knowledgeable about all the items on the menu**. Diners expect you to be able to discuss ingredients, answer questions and possibly recommend appropriate wines.
- **Anticipate your customers' needs**. Nothing's worse than a server who simply serves the food and then neglects the follow-up visits to the table.
- **Never leave anything in front of an unhappy customer**. Many servers make the mistake of discussing an offending dish with a diner without removing it first. You can easily turn this situation around and not jeopardize your tip by quickly apologizing, removing the item immediately, then returning with a replacement…on the house, of course.
- When presenting the check to the customer, do it professionally and efficiently. Many servers offer the bill, then seem to disappear. If the diner is ready to pay, it's your job to take the payment quickly. Says Eaton, "When people want to leave, they're ready to leave, so presenting the bill is critical to the meal. It's the last thing diners will remember about you in the restaurant.
- **Consider the personal touch**. Depending on the type of restaurant, you can add such extras as a happy face or a "Thank You" on the back of the bill. Patrons of family-style restaurants often warm to these personal touches.
- **Continue to educate yourself**. Spending time in restaurants noted for their service helps you become a better server.

As the restaurant industry has changed and become more professional, so too has the role of the server. Being a server, says Eaton, is not what it used to be. "Younger people coming up now are much more professional because of the rising status of the service industry." That professionalism is bound to pay off in higher tips for the best performers.

BODY LANGUAGE TIPS

To boost your confidence before an important meeting, replace your smart phone with a newspaper

Most business professionals I coach understand the importance of projecting confident body language during an important meeting, a job interview, say, or a key sales pitch, but few realize that how they sit while waiting in the reception area has everything to do with their initial impression.

Research shows that holding your body in expansive "high power" poses (standing tall with shoulders pulled back, widening your stance, spreading your arms to expand into space) raises testosterone (the hormone linked to power and self-confidence) and lowers the levels of the stress hormone, cortisol. This hormonal effect is actually reversed, the researchers discovered, when you contract yourself physically, (hunch your shoulders, tuck your chin down, etc.) assuming postures that make you look defensive and lacking in confidence.

Now picture yourself in the reception area where you are waiting for that important meeting. Are you bent over your smart phone, with your elbows pulled into your waist and your shoulders hunched? Or are you sitting up straight, feet firmly on the floor, arms spread wide holding an open newspaper? And, when you are called into the meeting, which of those two hormones is dominating your body chemistry?

To spot a liar, look out for these four "the tell-tale" signals

Non-verbal cues to all kinds of unconscious giveaways tend to occur in clusters - a group of movements, postures and actions that collectively point to a particular state of mind. This is crucially true of dishonesty, where one specific cluster of nonverbal signals has been proven statistically to be a highly accurate indicator of deception. These are: hand touching, face touching, crossed arms, and leaning away. According to research conducted atNortheastern University, if you see these "Telltale Four" being displayed together, watch out!

To make a difficult task seem easier, smile.

Charles Garfield, the author of Peak Performance, once coached the Russian Olympic weight-lifting team. Garfield noticed that when team members lifted to exhaustion, they would invariably grimace at the painful effort. In an experiment, he encouraged the athletes to smile when they got to that point of exhaustion. This seemingly minor difference enabled them to add 2-3 more reps to their performance.

No matter the task, when you grimace or frown while doing it, you are sending your brain the message, "This is really difficult. I should stop." The brain then responds by sending stress chemicals into your bloodstream. And this creates a vicious circle: the more stressed you are, the more difficult the task becomes.

Conversely, when you smile, your brain gets the message, "It's not so bad. I can do this!"

To reach an agreement, send early engagement signals.

Over the years, I've noticed that parties are more likely to reach an agreement if they begin a negotiation by displaying engaged body language (smiling, nodding, mirroring, open gestures, etc.). Interestingly, that positive result is the same whether the display was the product of an unconscious reaction or a strategic decision.

To encourage collaboration, rearrange your office.

Projecting power, authority, and status may be a key part of your nonverbal strategy to impress potential clients, customers, and investors - and if it is, then arranging your office space as a visual symbol of your and your company's brand can be a crucial part of that strategy.

When it comes to building collaboration within your staff, however, status and authority cues can send conflicting, distinctly unwanted messages. If creating a collaborative culture is essential to meeting your business objectives, then you might want to rearrange your office to reflect this. For example, seating people directly across from your desk (especially if their chair is smaller and lower than yours) places them in a competitive (and disadvantageous) position. Instead, try putting the visitor's chair at the side of your desk, or creating a conversation area (chairs of equal size set around a small table or at right angles to each other) to encourage a feeling of informality, equality, and partnership.

To reduce resistance, hand out your business card.

People who are defensive, guarded or resistant may protectively fold their arms across their chests. And when you see that gesture coupled with crossed legs, you can be fairly sure that (a) you aren't making a very positive impression, and that (b) what you're saying isn't being listened to very closely.

To automatically neutralize this kind of resistance in a one-on-one encounter, you could offer the individual a cup of coffee or tea. You could hand out your business card, brochure, or product sample. With a large audience you could ask questions that invite people to raise their hands ("How many of you have had previous training in nonverbal communication techniques?" "How many of you have never thought of body language as a leadership tool?") It doesn't matter which strategy you choose, just as long as people are obliged to change their postures, to uncross their arms and legs, in order to respond to you. Because body positions influence attitude, the mere act of unwinding a resistant posture will begin to subvert the resistance, itself.

To maximize your authority, curb your enthusiasm.

If you are an extrovert, you most likely make a favorable first impression - because we are drawn to passionate people whose emotions are easily read. But when your communication style lacks of nuance and subtlety, your over-exuberance can overwhelm (or exhaust) an audience. So in situations where you want to maximize your authority - minimize your movements. Take a deep breath, bring your gestures down to waist level, and pause before making a key point. When you appear calm and contained, you look more powerful.

To defuse a tense situation, realign your body more congenially.

Often strong verbal argument comes from a person's need to be heard and acknowledged. If you physically align yourself with that person (sitting or standing shoulder to shoulder facing the same direction), you will defuse the situation. And, by the way, a move that will escalate the argument is to square your body to the other person or to move in closer. This is especially true when dealing with men. Two men speaking will angle their bodies slightly, while two women will stand in a more "squared up" position - a stance that most men perceive as confrontational.

To "seal the deal," make a positive last impression.

After you've settled on a price, signed the contract, or accepted the job offer, remember to make a winning exit: Stand tall, shake hands warmly, make eye contact, smile, say "thank you," and leave your counterpart with the impression that you are someone he or she should look forward to dealing with in the future.

If you feel the need to improve your own body language, let your team know you're doing it.

I often coach leaders on using more inclusive body language to help create a collaborative work environment. If this is one of your New Year's resolutions, be upfront with your staff by saying, "I'm going through some training and I want to make positive changes in how I connect with others." That way your team will be looking for changes and will most likely understand what you are trying to achieve.

CHAPTER 12

Personality Development and Public Relations

PERSONALITY DEVELOPMENT

A new born baby is considered a tabula rasa, an empty sheet or an empty tablet. As he grows up he begins to fill up his sheet by gathering experiences to the place where he live. He begins to make his life and begins to mold his identity. In order to cope with anything outside the womb personality is the one of the major requirement.

Personality is the sum total of the qualities and characteristics of a person as shown in her manner of walking, dressing and her attitudes, interest and ways of reacting to other people. It refers to all the factors within the person that influence his characteristics, ways of behaving, thinking and feeling. It is your image on others. It is also typical pattern of thinking, feeling and behaviors that make a person unique.

Aspects of an Individual's Personality

1. **Physical aspect** - This includes the mode of dressing, manner of walking, posture, body build, health, complexion and facial expression.

2. **Intellectual/Mental aspect** - refers to intellectual capacity. How person talks, the range of ideas he expresses, and the things he talks about, as well as his values and mental alertness give evidence of his mental capacity.
3. **Emotional aspect** - A person's emotional makeup is shown in his likes and dislikes, whether he is aggressive or docile, how he responds when things become difficult, how quickly he is given to anger, whether he can take a job or not. Emotional behavior is interrelated with others aspect as child's growth. As he grows older, His emotions become differentiated.
4. **Social aspect** - This is seen in how people conducts himself with other people and how well he observes the rules of etiquette that govern society. Social attitudes and behavior are affected by physiological conditions and changes, mental alertness, [illegible] the extent of emotional maturity.

Factors Affecting Social Development

The social development of an individual is affected by several factors such as:

Socio-economic status

The higher the socio economic status, the higher is the cultural background of family members.

Level of maturity

The child will determine the level of assimilation he can do, given a social situation. A psychologists state, the higher the intelligence, the higher is the level of maturity of the individual.

Family cultural background

The family as the basic unit of society provides the laboratory for the socialization of the child. The style of life in the areas of socialization is a strong determinant for a child's foundation as far as social development is concern.

5. **Value system** - This includes a person's attitudes, values, beliefs and philosophy in life. This aspect referred to us as character. It shown in the way we judge whether our actions and actions of others are right or wrong.

6. **Spiritual aspect** - is the consciousness of the higher values in life. Religions expresses spiritual value

Components of Personality

1. **Habits** - are actions so often repeated at regular intervals until they become fixed characteristics.

   EX: going to church every Sunday, brushing one's teeth after every meal etc...

2. **Attitudes** - are certain ways of viewing things as ingrained, acquired, and developed through the years of exposure to man's family, school, and community.

3. **Interest** - is that natural inclination to focus one's concern towards a specific area of work.

4. **Values** - Are ways of upholding certain priorities in accordance with the hierarchy of needs by Abraham Maslow.

5. **Principles** - are guides to a person in making Judgement. The individual is consistent in his application of these principles which are in consonance with his norms of morality.

Personality Differences

1. **Heredity** - process of transmitting biological traits from parent to offspring through genes. It is also refers to the inherited characteristics of an individual, including traits such as height, eye color or blood type.

2. **Environment** - This consist of our family, school, church social group and other group with whom we interact from the very beginning. Each group put pressure on us and we behave in certain ways as result of being these groups. Our behavior changes with each situation and with the people we are with.

3. Experiences - These consist of everything we do or get in touch with. In everything that we are exposed whether physical, emotional or social experiences.

Reasons for Studying personality

Through our understanding of our own personalities of our fellowmen that will spell the differences between success and failure in our dealings with others. The study of this should result to our attempts to improve our own personality as well as to understand others so that we can adjust to them and have harmonious relations with them.

Reasons for Developing Personality

The development of our personality is our great responsibility. Some reasons why there is a need for developing personality are:

1. **Social acceptance** - it is the third need in the Filipino hierarchy of needs. The desire to be treated in accordance with one's status.
2. **Self-satisfaction** - a happy person meets the bad temper and unkind dispositions of others with understanding and good humor.
3. **Self-confidence** - elicits positive feelings which are necessary for mental health. We develop negative feelings like feelings of inferiority when we are aware that are personality is not as good as of others.
4. **To keep ourselves on the job** - personality has a great deal to do with holding a job.

Developing One's Personality

Although heredity sets the limit of one's development in personality, the environment provides the greater influence. The individual determines how he can maximize the development of his personality though the opportunities available to him in:

1. **Self awareness** - Indicates what kind of person you are. Our nature should be openly accepted by us so that our baseline data is actual and realistic.
2. **Assessment of personal asset and liabilities** - based on the factors such as intelligence, talents, industriousness, resourcefulness, flexibilities, and physical attractiveness.
3. **Personal growth** - can take off from self-awareness and personal asset and liabilities. Growing and learning continuously and consistency means total development.
4. **Personal effectiveness** - means how useful you are, not only to yourself but also to other people. "No one is an island", as a saying goes. One cannot live alone in a room and exempt himself from problems and challenges in society.

Techniques in Developing Personality

There are four steps to developing personality. These are the following:

1. Realize that improvement is needed.
2. Have a strong motive or desire to improve.
3. Take an inventory or make a checklist of strong and weak points of what is to be improved.
4. Have a step-by step procedure.

Some Tips to Develop the Personality

1. **Be a better listener:** Take time to listen with others story.
2. **Read more and expand your interest**: The more you read and cultivate new interest, the more interesting you are to others. When you meet new people it gives you the opportunity to share what you know and to exchange your views with them.
3. **Be a good conversationalist:** This relates to how much you read and know. Once you have much to contribute, learn how to talk about it with others.

4. **Have an opinion**: There is nothing more tiresome than trying to talk to someone who has no opinion on anything. A conversation has nowhere to go if you have nothing to expound on. However if you have an uncommon point of view or different opinion, you are interesting and stimulating to be in the company.

5. **Meet new people**: Make the effort to meet new people especially these unlike you. It not only expose you to different cultures an alternative ways of doing things. It broadens your horizons.

6. **Be yourself**: The next most tiresome thing after having no opinions is trying to be something you're not. Molding yourself in order to fit in, or be accepted, usually backfires. Since each of us is unique, expressing that unique is what makes us interesting. Attempting to be a carbon copy of some else not only falls flat, but reveals a lack of authenticity.

7. **Have a positive outlook and attitude**: Who wants to be around people who are negative, complain a lot, or have nothing good to say? In fact, most of us run when we see coming. Instead, be kind the nothing of upbeat person who lights up a room with you energy when we enter it. Do it by looking for the best in people and things. Smile warmly, spread good cheer and enliven others with your presence.

8. **Be fun and see the humorous side of life**: Everyone enjoys the company of someone who makes them laugh or smile. Look for the humorous or quirky side in a situation - there always one. When you are fun and lighthearted people are naturally attracted to you

9. **Be supportive of others:** Be supportive is probably the most endearing quality you can integrate you're your personality. Just as you yourself welcome it, be the support for others when they need it. We all love a cheerleader in our corner; someone who is encouraging, believes in us and helps pick us up when we're down

10. **Have Integrity and treat other people with respect**: Being honest and true to your word will bring you the admiration, respect and gratitude of others. Nothing improves a person's personality more than integrity and respect- respect others as well as respect yourself.

Beauty

This is the innate quality of a person. it also a way of being a manner of acting and a way of looking. To achieved balanced beauty the inner and outer must be blend to be joined by an ability to love and to be loved, by an awareness and curiosity about life, by intelligence and happiness, social grace and by self-expressions through all bodily movements - beauty is made, not born.

Outer beauty - People meet the outer you before they are able to meet the inner you.

- The outer packaging - consist of physical beauty and general appearance through clothing, accessories, make-up and hair style as well as shape and condition of the body.
- Personal attractiveness and the outer behavior, poise and education.
- Total image that determines just how handsome or beautiful a person is.
- Physical attractiveness, which includes physical factors, such as health, youthfulness, facial symmetry and complexion.

Inner beauty - To think is to be beautiful.

- An attitude by which to live and an image to project.
- It requires self-analysis, goal setting, commitment discipline and perseverance.
- Learn to recognize strength and weakness, the good and bad qualities and then decide what to be done.
- Inner beauty is calm, serene, optimistic, poised and self-confident which will be reflected in posture, face and voice.

Liking Yourself

It is essential to be beauty is to like and love yourself. Respect and love your unique self. It is only when you begin to love yourself that you will become an interesting person. The rewards of these are outward poise and inward confidence. Confidence brightens our eyes, strengthens our posture and brings a smile our lips.

Liking yourself doesn't mean you're full of pride, it simply means you accept yourself as the person God created you to be. When you start to like yourself, other people begin to like you too. We all need changes in our behavior, but accepting ourselves as God's creation is vital to our progress in becoming an emotionally healthy person.

CHAPTER 13

Personality Traits

PERSONALITY TRAITS AS ANTECEDENTS OF EMPLOYEE PERFORMANCE

Both researchers and industry practitioners are in agreement that in service industry, employee personality plays an important influence on the company's service quality, customer service skills, and overall performance of service providers, which in turn influences customer satisfaction, loyalty and ultimately organizational success. Employee personality is closely linked with organizational performance through its effect on employees' behavior, attitudes and service performance. There have been many researches on the role of personality traits as human behavior predictors.

LINK BETWEEN ORGANIZATIONAL EFFECTIVENESS AND EMPLOYEES' ATTITUDES AND BEHAVIOURS IN HOSPITALITY INDUSTRY

The three key characteristics of service industry that make employees' attitudes and behaviors critical are:

- **Intangibility of services**: in the absence of a tangible product, quality of employee-customer interaction becomes significant determinant of service quality and customer satisfaction.

- **Heterogeneity**· Involvement of humans makes services variable in nature, making standardization, productivity and consistency much more difficult to attain in hospitality organizations. Thus up to a large extent service quality and customer satisfaction would depend on the ability, drive and willingness of personnel.
- **Inseparability of individual with the organization**: In a hotel, the company's personnel personify and represent the organization. They help to form the image of the hotel in the customer's eye.

Previous studies have strongly suggested connections between profits of organizations and their employees' market orientation, especially among service-oriented industries. In context of hospitality industry, some of the organizational outcomes that have a direct link with employees' attitude and behavior are:

- Service quality
- Customer satisfaction
- Financial performance
- Competitive success
- Turnover.

The attitude and behavior of the employees is also dependent on several factors like their personality, training received, culture of the organization etc.

In this chapter, you will learn about personality traits, including the most widely accepted model of classifying personality traits, the Big Five factors.

BIG FIVE PERSONALITY MODEL

Attempting to understand and classify what makes people who they are has been a longstanding challenge in the world of personality psychology. Numerous theories and models have been developed over the years to better understand aspects of human personality. Most trait theory models attempt to accurately describe aspects of personality.

The focus of this lesson is on the Big Five personality traits. In psychology, the 'Big Five' is a term used to describe the five broad traits of human personality. In current practice, it is sometimes used interchangeably with the term 'five-factor model.'

Each of the traits, or factors, identified as the Big Five are independent of each other and account for the infinite number of unique aspects that comprise human personality. Understanding each of the Big Five factors will help you better grasp the concept of personality traits.

The Big Five personality traits are:

- Openness
- Conscientiousness
- Extraversion
- Agreeableness
- Neuroticism

An easy way to remember the Big Five is to remember thc word 'OCEAN.' The first letter of each trait creates the word ocean.

The Big Five traits have been subjected to rigorous testing over the past several decades. The research continues to support the notion that we all possess each of the five personality characteristics to some degree. And even though we share only five common personality traits, the possible combinations, or personality types, are endless when you consider the varying degrees of each trait. For example, not all of us are equally agreeable or neurotic.

Big Five Personality Traits

Now that we have identified each of the Big Five personality traits, let's take a look at each one individually.

Openness refers to traits, such as how inclined someone is to conform to societal or cultural norms, how concretely or abstractly someone thinks about things, and how open or resistant someone is to change. A person who is a creative thinker and always looking for ways to do things better would likely score high on measures of openness.

Conscientiousness has to do with a person's degree of organization, level of discipline, and how prone he or she is to taking risks. The college student who never misses a class and has a 4.0 GPA would probably prove to have a high degree of conscientiousness as measured on a personality assessment.

Extraversion is a personality characteristic that describes things like how social a person is or how warm and loving they tend to be. Extraverts are people who would typically prefer to go out to a party with lots of friends, as opposed to stay in and watch a movie with one or two friends.

Agreeableness takes into account how kind, dependable, and cooperative a person is. People who score high on scales of agreeableness are typically more interested in doing things for the common good, as opposed to fulfilling their own self-interests.

Neuroticism is the tendency to experience negative emotions, such as anger, anxiety, or depression. It is sometimes called emotional instability, or is reversed and referred to as emotional stability. According to researchers theory of personality, neuroticism is interlinked with low tolerance for stress or aversive stimuli. Those who score high in neuroticism are emotionally reactive and vulnerable to stress. They are more likely to interpret ordinary situations as threatening, and minor frustrations as hopelessly difficult. Their negative emotional reactions tend to persist for unusually long periods of time, which means they are often in a bad mood. For instance, neuroticism is connected to a pessimistic approach toward work, confidence that work impedes personal relationships, and apparent anxiety linked with work. Furthermore, those who score high on neuroticism may display more skin conductance reactivity than those who score low on neuroticism. These problems in emotional regulation can diminish the ability of a person scoring high on neuroticism to think clearly, make decisions, and cope effectively with stress. Lacking contentment in one's life achievements can correlate with high neuroticism scores and increase one's likelihood of falling into clinical depression. Moreover, individuals high on neuroticism tend to experience more negative life events, but neuroticism also changes in response to positive and negative life experiences.

At the other end of the scale, individuals who score low in neuroticism are less easily upset and are less emotionally reactive. They tend to be calm, emotionally stable, and free from persistent negative feelings. Freedom from negative feelings does not mean that low scorers experience a lot of positive feelings.

Neuroticism is similar but not identical to being neurotic in the Freudian sense (i.e. neurosis.) Some psychologists prefer to call neuroticism by the term emotional stability to differentiate it from the term neurotic in a career test.

CONCLUSION

Given the fact that personality plays such a significant part of a hospitality organization's performance, it seems only natural that personality testing should be a fundamental part of hospitality recruitment process. Hospitality organizations can significantly increase their organizational effectiveness and reduce attrition by using personality tests to select employees that are predisposed to be service oriented. This will cut down costly and time-consuming interviews of every job applicant and also help in training need analysis.

The most important conclusion of this study was that the personality based competencies can be used to select high performance hospitality personnel. Specifically, customer orientation and ability to handle stress stimulated high performance behaviors in employees. Having said that, personality traits alone should not be the means on which to base selection decisions, instead, hospitality organizations can utilize personality testing to complement the traditional methods of screening job applicants, such as interviews and job applications, thereby increasing their employee performance while minimizing costs.

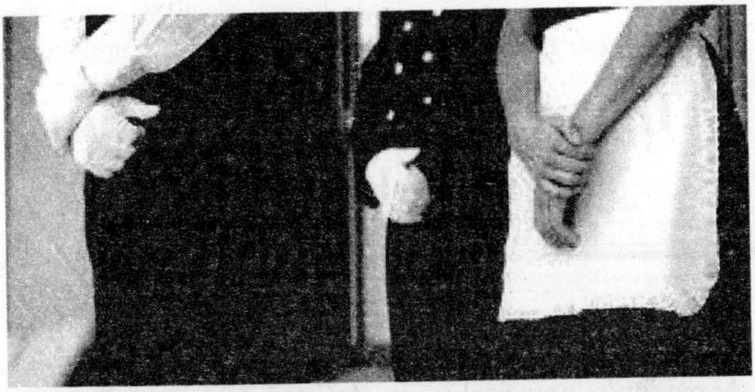

CHAPTER 14

Importance of Personality Development

A person's personality is defined by their characteristics, behaviors, thoughts, and feelings. These aspects start developing during childhood, and are strengthened and molded as the person grows into adulthood.

A very important thing you need to remember is that your personality, regardless of what it is now, can develop and evolve. The significance of this understanding is that you can still do something about your personality today, which means that if you think your personality needs to be changed or improved, then you can make this happen.

Why is personality development important?

The following points will help you understand why.

Your Personality Will Help You Build Strong Personal Relationships

Have you ever wondered why some people have lots of friends while others do not? Or why others can easily adapt to any social gathering while others cannot? The difference is largely due to the type of personality these people have. While some people have a very likeable personality, some are rather intimidating and difficult which causes others to avoid them. Try to observe parties and you will notice how those who are always smiling and going out of their way to talk others are the life of the party, while there are also those who prefer to stay in one corner, all by their lonesome selves.

In family life, how you deal with your spouse, your parents, or your children also has something to do with the kind of person you are. Although the love of a family is unconditional, there are certainly times when challenges arise, and how you deal with each one affects the relationship you will have with your family.

If you are too shy to speak when in a group, then this only means you lack self-esteem and confidence. If your relationship with your family is not too well, then it only means you lack communication and trust among each other. All these can be changed if you strive to improve and develop your personality.

Your Personality Will Dictate Success in Your Career

In the workplace, it is quite common to experience difficulties, from something as simple as beating traffic to stressful ones such as meeting project deadlines, as well as maintaining good relationships with your bosses and colleagues. Though majority of us have the mental capacity to handle the responsibilities bestowed on us, we lack a high level of emotional intelligence which is considered just as important to get the job done.

As you might be well-aware of, emotional intelligence and personality go hand in hand. This is why personality development holds a very vital role in a person's ability to succeed in whatever careerhe chooses to take. If you are easily frustrated, without the capability to handle stress brought about by work-related events, then it will be easy for you to give up during difficult times.

Since personality also entails knowing how to relate with others, knowing how to communicate effectively, and even how to dress appropriately, it is instrumental in helping us climb the echelon of success.

Personality Development Helps You Improve

Dorothy Jongeward and Muriel James, in their much talked about book "Born to Win," talked about how each individual has been born to be a winner. However, in the course of development, from infancy to adulthood, negligence towards our own potentials took a toll on our progress, and as a result, we are no longer able to use our unique traits to their fullest.

The good news is that with personality development, we can do something about this. No matter how ordinary we think we are, we can polish our traits and behaviors and shine through. We can transform our personality into one that aims to succeed in any aspect of our lives.

These are just some of the reasons why personality development is very important. In a nutshell, developing one's own personality addresses the problems we face both at home and at work, helping us become successful in every endeavor we engage ourselves in.

It is never too late to change. No matter how young or old you are, whatever level you may be in your career, you can still do something to achieve a better, more desirable personality.

THE POWER OF BODY LANGUAGE

Understanding body language does more than improve relationships. You will get insight into the thoughts and feelings of those around you. Because it is not a conscious form of communication, people betray themselves in their body language. Body language is powerful in several ways.

Power of Body Language: It is honest: Body language conveys truth, even when words do not.

- Creates self awareness: Understanding body language helps you identify your own actions
- that hinder success. Understand feelings: Body language shows feelings and motive such as aggression,

- submission, deception, etc. Use these as cues to your communication. Enhance listening and communication skills: Paying attention to body language makes
- someone a better listener. Hear between the words spoken to what is being said.

CHAPTER 15

Soft Skills for Hospitality Industry

INTRODUCTION

The Introductory unit on Soft Skills for hospitality industry has highlighted the importance of soft skills. The unit has explained in detail one of the most important soft skills i.e. Communication. In this unit we shall study other important soft skills that will help you to earn an edge in your personal, social as well as professional life. In fact these soft skills are directly related to your personality and will help you to develop a personality suitable for travel and tourism industry.

DEFINING PERSONALITY

Before we start defining personality, let's have a trip down the memory lane and remember two of your neighbourhood or old school friends with whom you have interacted.

One liked by everyone. She/he makes friend very quickly, smiles and greets people. Always a favourite student of teachers as well as favourite of all relatives and neighbours. Everyone enjoys talking to and being around him/her. The other one always complains and has trouble keeping friends for long. She/he bosses his little siblings at home. Always a troublemaker at school and neighbourhood. All kids complain that she/ he picks up the fight. Even in the school she/he is never able to be a part of sports team. What is the difference between the two? The difference is their different personalities.

The concept of personality is one of the major topics of interest for some of the top psychologist. In this unit we will define it from the view point of social attractiveness of an individual not from the scientific view point.

The word 'personality' has its roots in Latin word 'persona' which means a mask. In old days in order to represent qualities of a typical character of drama on stage masks were used.

Personality in general terms means the unique set of qualities (i.e. physical, mental and emotional attitudes, values, interests) that make you different from others. Personality is actually how you present yourself to others and how people define you. Your personality is everything about you.

Oxford Dictionary defines personality as the combination of characteristics or qualities that form an individual's distinctive character.

Here the question which tickles our mind is that what all comes under personality? Encyclopaedia Britannica describes personality includes way of thinking, feeling, and behaving. Personality embraces moods, attitudes, and opinions and is most clearly expressed in interactions with other people. It includes behavioural characteristics that distinguish one person from another and that can be observed in people's relations to the environment and to the social group.

The case of two friends discussed in the beginning of this unit also highlights the fact that in simple term personality means social skills. The difference in their social skills like one is friendly, collaborator and other is domineering, troublemaker brings out the differences in their personality. Thus personality is being used as a general label for the amount of social skill and finesse.

1.3 Determinants of Personality:

Each individual has unique personality. Have you ever think how personality is shaped? There are certain factors which shape personality of individual called determinants of personality. A survey of works of different psychologist brings forward a plethora of determinants of personality. Here to keep things basic we will discuss the generic determinants of personality. These are:

1. Heredity,
2. Culture,
3. Family Background,
4. Our Experiences through Life,
5. And the People we interact with

Heredity

Oxford dictionary describes heredity as the passing on of physical or mental characteristics genetically from one generation to another. We inherit certain traits, such as the colour of our eyes, the shape of our face and body from our father, grandfather and great grandfather. Mainly these four aspects of personality we inherit-body build physical attractiveness, physical defects and health conditions from our ancestors. Most people are born with a mixture of traits. Heredity forms your basic personality. And then the effects of our environment add to our personality development.

Environment includes everything and everyone around us. Environment may help bring out certain traits more than others. The other four determinants we will study now constitute our environment.

Culture

Culture can be defined as the ideas, customs, and social behaviour of a particular people or society. We learn values and inclination from our culture and it shapes our behaviour. Behaviour defines our personality. Thus people born in different cultures tend to develop different types of personalities. In India we can find diversity in cultural backgrounds and each culture has some general features that highlight personality of people of that culture in general.

For example, people from Gujarat are more enterprising, people from Haryana are daring and people from Bengal are creative and have great intellectual bend. Also it is not necessary that all people belonging to a culture showcase the similar personality trait but in general according to culture the dominating personality trait is found in majority of people.

Family Background

Family is the smallest unit of society. Family is a group of people related by blood or marriage. The foremost influencer after heredity to shape personality of a baby is family. Many aspects of family like background and education of parents, socio-economic status, the number of children in the family and birth order and extended members of the family such as uncles and aunts influence the shaping of personality to a considerable extent. Think once your liking -disliking, way of problem solving, way of expressing your feelings etc. all are one in other way a reflection of what you have learned from your family.

Experiences in Life

One of the famous quotes by Julio Caesar - "Experience is the teacher of all things" best explains this determinant of personality. Your personality might have kindness as a trait but repeated experience in your life where you felt cheated due to kindness can influence your this personality trait for future. Suppose three such incidents happened to you with three different individuals in the past few months where you have given money but they never came back to you. What is the probability that you would trust another person who comes and asks you for a loan tomorrow? Rather low, one would think. Thus, certain personality characteristics are moulded by frequently occurring positive or negative experiences in life.

People We Interact With

"A Person is known by the company he or she keeps" is a common proverb. We interact with an array of people in our life like - neighbours, teachers, classmates, schoolmates, friends, cousin, colleagues, boss and even strangers etc. People who are alike us in attitude and value we persuade them and associate with them. Even we change our behaviours to get accepted and associated with them whom we like. For instance, we may have to become less aggressive, more cooperative to work successfully in a team etc. Thus, our personality becomes shaped throughout our lives by at least some of the people and groups we interact with.

In summary, our personality is a function of both heredity and environment (external factors) that shape it and keep it shaping.

For example: the comfort of five star hotel room like high quality bed and linen, best of antiques in room, international quality good food, costly furniture etc. are useless if the people serving in hotel lack professional serving attitude, manners, communication skills and have poor hygiene sense etc. Thus, essentially we can say that to have a happy customer at the end of the day the people serving in hospitality industry should have:

1. Positive Attitude to work
2. Well Groomed Personality to create first impression.
3. Social Etiquettes & Telephonic Etiquettes
4. Professional Body Language.

Thus, eventually these above - mentioned areas turn into the key aspects of personality which require to be developed to have a desired personality for hospitality industry. In succeeding pages we will study these areas to learn how to develop personality for hospitality industry.

Power of Positive Attitude

Researchers have proved that a person who focuses on positive side of anything, be a person, event or object are happier, live longer and become successful in their life as compared to those who have negative attitude. The statement of the most influential

American Philosopher William James further strengthens this fact. He had said that "Pessimism leads to weakness, optimism to power."

The power of positive attitude has been reinforced by a study of Harvard University also which says that the main driving force to get a good job in eighty-five percent cases is attitude and remaining fifteen percent is the technical know-how. Thus positive attitude enhances our personality traits and lifts our personality to a more attractive level both in personal as well as professional arena of life. Furthermore following points highlight the power of positive attitude:

1. A positive attitude triggers our enthusiasm.
2. A positive attitude enhances our creativity.
3. A positive attitude makes good things happen.

Positive Work Attitude

Till now we have understood that a positive attitude is a virtue for one's personality. But to be always positive at your workplace whether school, office or society is not very easy. Every day we face many ups and downs especially at work place. Sometimes we feel positive and sometimes we feel negative. It becomes necessary for us to handle these ups and downs positively. How we can do this? Following strategies can help us to have a positive work attitude irrespective of any circumstances at work place:

1. **Examine Your Attitude Regularly**: Every day one should examine his/her attitude towards work, co-workers and boss whether it's positive or negative. If it's positive do your co-workers and boss perceive it positively or not? Also if it is negative then what are the reasons behind it? When you question yourself like this , you will definitely find a problem, and if problem is there it must have a solution. Then try to solve this problem by adjusting you attitude or if required by even changing your attitude from negative to positive.

2. **Balance Work with Personal Life**: Another strategy is to have a mix of fun and work. For this you should establish your priorities in life. Priorities mean something that is more important than other things. At home family should be priority and at work place office work should be priority. We should not think about work when at home and also should not allow family concerns disturb our office work. Setting priorities and meeting them successfully make our attitude more focused and positive.
3. **Focus on the Positive**: Always focus on your strengths and successes even if you are not able to be successful in all aspects of your work and in your relationships in the job.
4. **Communicate**: Communication is lifeline of all relationship. When communication stops miscommunication begins and negativity spreads. Thus it is very important to communicate effectively as well as listen patiently. You should be able to make other understand what you want to say and at the same time understand properly what they want to communicate. Practice good listening and communication skills every day.
5. **Turn Unexpected Changes into Opportunity**: Change is inevitable and change always bring friction. Human beings soon adapt themselves to a routine and any change in it brings negative reactions.

   Example - Change of Boss or co-worker or job profile. But one can learn to accept change and remain positive. Focus on what one can learn from this change and see the change as an opportunity to learn new things and grow.
6. **Educate Yourself**: One should be well-versed in one's job only then one can enjoy it. One should put effort to educate oneself in all areas where improvements are required. Even if you know your job well always try to update your knowledge and learn new things. Be a lifelong learner. The more you learn, the more confident you will be.

7. **Maintain Your Interest**: A new job means new challenges and many new things to learn. But with passage of time the challenges become routine affairs and you start feeling bored and negativity increases. Thus, you should look for ways to regain the interest. Take new initiatives and invent new ideas for doing routine tasks.

8. **Maintain a Sense of Humour**: Humour can help you to overcome tension at work and see the lighter side of the things. Having a sense of humour does not mean joking or clowning around. Having a sense of humour means developing the ability to see positive things and lessen the tension in environment. The famous quote of 34th President of U.S.A Dwight D. Eisenhower reemphasizes the importance of humour - "A sense of humour is part of the art of leadership, of getting along with people, of getting things done."

9. **Take Care of Your Health**: There is a direct relationship between healthy habits, productivity and positive attitude. A person who has habit of exercising daily will definitely have good health and high productivity at workplace. Such individual will have high positive energy and attitude towards everyone in the office. But if you sleep very late, do not exercise in the morning, have low level of energy at office definitely your productivity will be less and negative attitude will increase in you, your boss and also co-workers. Thus poor health habits can affect your job performance and your attitude.

10. **Dress for Success**: Last but not the least. How you dress and how you carry yourself reflects your attitude. In fact this is one of the most important areas of personality development and also our next important topic under study. This point is explained in later pages as a separate topic.

Thus, the above mentioned ten strategies help us to maintain positive attitude and thus can make our personality advantageous for hospitality industry.

CREATING FIRST IMPRESSION AND GROOMING

Often you have heard the famous phrase - 'First impression is the last impression'. Have you ever thought what this impression is, how it is formed, why first impression is so important and how one can make first impression extraordinarily? In this section we shall try to answer these questions.

According to Oxford dictionary impression is an idea, feeling, or opinion about something or someone, especially one formed without conscious thought or on the basis of little evidence. As the definition highlights when we meet somebody for the first time without knowing much about other in totality we create an idea about him/her.

Also, the first impression becomes very important because the idea which is created lasts long. In fact a study by Harvard Business School social psychologist, Amy Cuddy, says that if in first few seconds of meeting we are able to show trustworthiness and confidence as leading trait of our personality then we earn a long lasting relationship. And these two traits are conveyed not on the basis of one's intelligence or experience, rather than on basis of one's attire and grooming level. Thus one has to work on these two aspects of one's personality to make first impression extraordinary.

ATTIRE /CLOTHING

Attire means the way we dress up. As we judge books by their covers similarly we judge people by their clothes. Also the way we dress up show our attitude towards life. It is very important to wear clothes which convey positive about us. But how we can do this especially in our work place?

The thumb rule is that we should adapt ourselves to the dress-code of the work place. When we follow the dress-code of the industry than we project an image which gel with the image and work-culture of the work-place.

In hospitality industry it is very important because the way we carry ourselves convey the image of the company as well as the quality of service. This is the reason why airline employees wear high quality formal clothes to reassure high quality of service. Thus, at the work place what we wear indicates towards our professionalism. Also two types of clothing are common in hospitality industry - Business Formals (generally Monday to Thursday) and Business Casual (generally Friday). The following two images give a description of types of business formals and business casuals prevalent in hospitality industry:

GROOMING

The second important area which helps you to create a first good impression is grooming. The Oxford dictionary defines grooming as a noun (derived from 'groom') which means to have a neat and tidy appearance. It is imperative to take care of your overall appearance which includes neatness and cleanliness of body and hair. It also includes how we manage accessories which we put up with our clothes like belt, shoes, purse, watch, jewellery etc. Daily grooming is a must -must especially for work place. Your health, as well as the health of others, depends on your practices of personal cleanliness. Also, if we are not well groomed then even the most costly clothes do not help a person to create a good impression. Overdo of make-up and use of accessories can destroy the most professional attire.

Thus, to have a true professional formal look at workplace one has to take care of many do's and do not's of dressing and grooming. The following general grooming tips help you to be professionally groomed:

1. **Hair**: Clean and neatly styled, no wet hair, no over the top colours or hairstyles. For Men go for a shorter haircut, and trim chest hair (no hair visible at the neckline!).
2. **Shoes**: Polished and in good condition.
3. **Nails**: Clean, trimmed, neatly manicured. For women no extreme colors or length.

4. **Cosmetics**: Makeup should be conservative, aim for a natural, polished look.
5. **Perfume/Cologne**: Use very little or not at all, clothes should be odour free (no smoke smell!)
6. **Facial Hair**: Clean shaven or trimmed very short and neat.
7. **Tattoos**: Cover all tattoos if possible. No Tattoo should be visible.
8. **Piercings**: Remove all facial and body piercings. For women one earring per ear and for Men no earrings allowed.
9. **Back-packs**: Do not take a back-pack to an on-site interview.
10. **Purse**: A small, conservative handbag or business tote bag is acceptable. Bag should coordinate with shoe colour.

The above details in attire and grooming when taken care of help you to create a positive professional first impression and in this way you half win your battle in the beginning.

BASIC SOCIAL ETIQUETTES

Another area which helps us to define and shape your personality is Social Etiquettes. Oxford dictionary defines it as 'the customary code of polite behaviour in society or among members of a particular profession or group.'

Etiquette when defined most simply means respect, good manners, and good behaviour we project in our social settings be it office, friends or family. It is not just each of these things, but it is all of these things rolled into one.

For the purposes of this unit, we will focus on two major areas of business etiquette: Work and telephone.

Work /Office Etiquette

These days office is the place where we spent more waking hours of a day as compared to our home. Office environment and office people have become a vital part of our life and shape our success in life. It has become imperative to treat our office people and office environment a notch better than family.

The following principles given by Myrna Hoover in her work Using Proper Etiquette can be utilized by office employees to show proper etiquette; they include all aspects of the work environment.

1. Be timely: To be punctual at work and meetings is an important attribute of one's personality. It shows that you value other's time. Also one should complete work assignments on time.
2. Be polite, pleasant, and courteous. Treat others the way you want to be treated.
3. Learn office politics. One should understand the story of office and role played by different employees. Utilize effective listening skills to discover appropriate office behaviour. Pay attention to the way things are done.
4. Understand the four unwritten rules of business:
    a. The Boss is the Boss: right or wrong, the boss always has the last word.
    b. Keep the boss informed. Good or bad, you don't want the boss to listen information mentioned from an inappropriate source.
    c. Never go over the boss' head without telling him or her first.
    d. Make your boss look good. Promotion and opportunities arise when you help the organization reach its goals.
5. Adopt a can-do attitude. This highlights the positivity of your personality. Those who accept challenges as opportunity can display creativity and become valuable.
6. Be flexible. Not necessary that everything that happens in the office is liked and accepted by you. Sometimes you can have

a difference of opinion about a change but at that time should have flexibility. By remaining flexible and implementing change, you gain a reputation as a cooperative employee.

7. Give credit to everyone who made a contribution to a project or event. In this way you earn good reputation and at the same time you will also enjoy credit by others.

8. Do not differentiate people by position or standing in a company.

Thus, by following more and more business etiquette you will be able to create a good impression about your personality. These visible signals are essential to your professional success.

BUSINESS TELEPHONE ETIQUETTE

Think of one day in your life without telephone. Out of all modes of communication the telephone is the one of the most useful tools in every day communication. It has been estimated that major percentage of today's business is conducted over the telephone, as it is an immediate means of communicating. Particularly in hospitality industry telephone is the most used way of communication with customer, supplier as well as with in office. The way telephone call is answered create the image of the company. One can enhance their professional reputation through polite and effective telephone manners. It has been proved that if we cannot handle telephone calls professionally then people think twice before doing business with the company. That's the reason these days companies have standard operating procedure of handling phone calls in which these aspects are most important:

1. Answering the call
2. Making the calls
3. Taking a Message
4. Leaving a Message

Answering the Telephone

- Answering promptly that is allowing no more than two or three rings before picking up the handset. An immediate response says a lot about you and promotes good public relations.
- Answering with a smile which the caller will hear it in your voice. A cheerful voice begets a happy caller or listener, and a favourable impression is created.
- Speaking in a warm, audible, clear voice at a moderate phase so that the caller can follow the conversation.
- Not eating, drinking, smoking or coughing while talking into the mouthpiece. If you have to cough, excuse yourself first, cover the mouthpiece and cough away from it.
- Always sound professional, pleased to hear from someone and ready to deal with their concerns.

Making Telephone Calls

- The impression you create on the telephone reflects not only your personality but also the image of your company, organisation or employer. Try to phone when you know it is convenient for the other person and confirm that they are able to speak.
- Always identify yourself and your company immediately. This information makes you sound confident and in control, and enhances your chances of being put through promptly to the person you're trying to reach.
- If you make a long distance call and the other person is not available, you should try again. Do not leave a message that the person should phone you.
- Answering with a smile which the caller will hear it in your voice. A cheerful voice begets a happy caller or listener, and a favourable impression is created.

When leaving a message

- Give full details so that the person who returns your call can get in touch with you.
- The first name and surname are important, as is the reason for the call.
- If you call wanting to offer or sell the person something, do not leave a message; rather phone back later. Ask when it will be convenient to speak to the person and call back at that time.

When taking a message

- Keep the following at hand at all times: a pen, a message book, a calendar and a dairy (in case appointments have to be made).
- Take messages carefully and write down all the details in your message book for the possible future reference.
- Note for whom the message is intended, plus the full name and title of the person who called. Ensure that you have the correct spellings of all names and surnames. Record the date and time of the call.
- Obtain their telephone number and code as well as the extension, and ask until what time their call can be returned.
- Note the name of the organisation or business they represent, as well as the purpose of the call.
- In the case of an urgent message, take the caller's home or cell phone number.
- For safety sake, leave the handwritten message on the person's desk.

Thus, when one handles this mode of communication effectively in office then problems are solved easily, productivity and customer satisfaction is achieved. Also, your positive image is created, professional worth increases in office as well as with customers.

POSITIVE BODY LANGUAGE

We have already studied body language and its components last year. It is the study of movements of our body parts like eyes, head, hands, legs, sitting style, walking style etc. called body language. It is also called Gestural Communication or Kinesics. It truly depicts the inner feeling going in our mind. We can fake our words to conceal our true inner feeling but our body movements convey it.

CONCLUSION

Personality development is a cautious and continous effort of individuals to inculcate attributes like positive attitude,etiquetts and positive body language in their personality so that they achieve new heights in Hospitality Indusrty.Hospitality industry is a people to people,intangible and glamours industry which demands professionals which have a right blend of hard skills and soft skills. This unit has described in the simplest way the importance of personality and how it is formed.It also explains that with our efforts we can develop our personality as desired. For it we need to develop positive attitude ,we need to take care of our looks and grooming and learn the etiquettes of work place and telephone handling. Further, learning of positive body language helps us to put up a charsmatic personality. All this makes us employable for hospitality industry and help us to achieve new heights in the hospitality industry.

CHAPTER 16

Communication and Listening Skills

INTRODUCTION

Communication is any means by which an individual relates experiences, ideas, knowledge, and feelings to another. Communication can be expressed through both speech and gestures. It is important that mentors know how to effectively communicate with mentees. This section is devoted to information and activities designed to develop active listening and communication skills effective for working with an adolescent population.

When establishing a mentoring relationship, it is important to create a comfortable communication environment. This can be done by using the theory of reciprocity. Following this theory enables mentors to control the flow and direction of a conversation by the rate at which information is revealed.

For example, if the mentor reveals something about him- or herself, the mentee would likely respond by revealing the same sort of information. This pattern tends to repeat. If at some point the mentee does not respond in kind, the pattern of the conversation should be redirected to make the mentee feel more comfortable. This type of interaction pattern fosters the development of trust in the mentoring relationship.

GUIDELINES FOR COMMUNICATION

To encourage the development of trust in the mentoring relationship:

- Make communication positive, clear, and specific.
- Recognize that each individual sees things from a different point of view.
- Be open and honest about your feelings and accept othersí feelings.
- Ask questions for clarification on an issue.
- Learn to listen. Allow time for the student to talk without interruptions.

These suggestions should be used as guidelines. There may be situations that require mentors to act differently.

ACTIVE LISTENING SKILLS

Active listening is an essential mentoring skill. One of the most common mistakes mentors can make is confusing "hearing" and "listening". Hearing is merely noting that someone is speaking. Listening, however, is making sense of what is heard and requires the individual to constantly pay attention, interpret, and remember what is heard. Hearing is passive; listening is active. The passive listener is much like a tape recorder. If the speaker is providing a clear message, the listener will probably get most of what is said. For mentors, this is not enough. They must be active listeners. Active listening requires the listener to hear the words and identify the feelings associated with the words. Mentors should be able to understand the speaker from his or her point of view. There are four essential requirements for active listening:

- Intensity
- Empathy
- Acceptance

- Willingness to take responsibility for completeness.

An active listener concentrates on what the speaker is saying. The human brain is capable of handling a speaking rate six times that of the average speaker. Thus, the listener must focus on the speaker. Tuning out distractions will increase listening ability.

Suggestions for Improving Active Listening Skills

1. **Make Eye Contact**: Lack of eye contact may be interpreted as disinterest or disapproval. Making eye contact with the speaker focuses attention, reduces the chance of distraction, and is encouraging to the speaker.
2. **Exhibit Affirmative Nods and Appropriate Facial Expressions**: The effective listener shows signs of being interested in what is said through nonverbal signs. Together with good eye contact, non-verbal expressions convey active listening.
3. **Avoid Distracting Actions or Gestures**: Do not look at other people, play with pens or pencils, shuffle papers, or the like. These activities make the speaker feel like the listener is not interested in what is being said.
4. **Ask Questions**: Questioning helps ensure clarification of what the speaker is saying, facilitates understanding, and lets the speaker know that the listener is engaged.
5. **Paraphrase**: Paraphrasing means restating what the individual has said in different words. This technique allows the listener to verify that the message was received correctly.
6. **Avoid Interrupting the Speaker**: Allow the speaker to complete his or her thought before responding, and do not anticipate what he/she will say.
7. Do Not Talk Too Much: Talking is easier than listening intently to someone else. An active listener recognizes that it is impossible to talk and listen acutely at the same time.

POSITIVE FEEDBACK

Mentors should focus on providing positive feedback. Negative feedback inhibits the mentee from talking freely and usually meets more resistance. Positive feedback, however, is typically met with acceptance. Suggestions for providing positive feedback:

- Focus on Specific Behaviors: Avoid vague, general statements like "You did a good job" or "That was a really bad decision." Instead, provide information that tells why you feel what you expressed. For instance, "You played a great game today. I liked the way you played defense."
- Keep Feedback Goal Oriented: Make sure statements are relevant to what the speaker is saying.
- Keep Feedback Well Timed: Providing immediate feedback is much more effective than comments given at a later time.
- Ensure Understanding: Just as it is important for listeners to understand the speaker, it is also important for listeners to be understood by the speaker. Asking the mentee to rephrase what has been said helps to ensure confirmation (Robbins, 1991).

Effective communication requires practice. By following the advice in this unit and finding opportunities to practice the skills with other mentors or with friends and family (e.g., creating activities that use specific skills), mentors, over time, should feel more comfortable with effective communication styles.

GUIDELINES OF COMMUNICATION

1. Make your communication positive, clear, and specific.
2. Recognize that each individual sees things from a different point of view.
3. Be open and honest about your feelings and accept othersí feelings.
4. Ask questions for clarification on an issue.

5. Learn to listen actively and allow time for the mentee to talk without interruption.

ESSENTIALS OF ACTIVE LISTENING

1. Intensity
2. Empathy
3. Acceptance
4. Recognizing responsibility for completeness.

WAYS TO IMPROVE ACTIVE LISTENING SKILLS

1. Make Eye Contact
2. Use Affirmative Nods and Appropriate Facial Expressions
3. Avoid Distracting Actions or Gestures
4. Ask Questions
5. Paraphrase
6. Avoid Interrupting the Speaker
7. Do Not Talk Too Much.

CHAPTER 17

Presentation Skills

MANAGING PRESENTATION NERVES

Your stomach is queasy, your palms are sweaty, and your mind has gone blank about your opening lines. What will you be like when you've been introduced and the room goes quiet? Are you doomed to presentation panic or paralysis, or can you overcome that debilitating nervousness and deliver a speech that wows the audience? (Or at least leaves them feeling satisfied?)

If you are like most people, then public speaking or presenting is one of your major fears. Yet these skills arc often called upon. It might not be to an audience of hundreds, but giving presentations to staff or even team members is a common enough occurrence. You owe it to yourself to develop some strategies and techniques to manage your nerves so you can concentrate on delivering an effective and engaging presentation.

Notice we didn't say to get rid of your nervousness. This is because presenting is not a natural activity; even the most practiced presenters get a bit nervous. The point is this: your nervous energy can be used to your advantage. When you are in a heightened state from the adrenaline that is being pumped into your body, you can use that energy to communicate enthusiastically, convincingly, and passionately. The key is to decrease your level of nervousness so you can use your energy on these positive activities, not on trying to control your nerves.

So, to harness your nervousness and bring it under control, there are six key tips to remember. These tips are all designed to help you focus on your audience and their needs rather than on yourself and how you are feeling. They all stem from one truism:

SIX STEPS TO CONQUERING YOUR PRESENTATION NERVES

Step 1 – Know Your Audience

Consult your audience before your presentation. The more confident you are that you are presenting them with useful and interesting material for them, the less nervous you will be overall. You really don't want your presentation to be a surprise. If it is, you lose complete control over the audience's reaction and that is a large factor in nervousness. So:

Define who your target audience is.

- Ask people who are representative of the audience what they expect from the presentation.
- Run your agenda by a few people to see if they think something is missing or is overkill.
- Consider contacting participants by email beforehand and asking them a few questions about what they expect.
- Greet audience members at the door and do a quick survey of why they are there and what they expect.

Step 2 – Know Your Material

Nothing is worse for nerves than trying to give a presentation on a topic you are not well prepared for. This doesn't mean you have to be an expert beforehand, but you'd better know it backwards on presentation day. And making sure you've understood your audience and their needs properly will help you ensure that your material is on target to meet their needs.

Another important point to remember is that you can't possibly cover everything you know in your presentation. That would probably be long and boring. So select the most pertinent points from your subject base and then supplement with other material if time allows.

Tip

To make your material interesting and memorable, include occasional questions to the audience to encourage audience participation. This enhances the learning experience and gives you a break from presenting. It also allows you deliver your information in a more conversational manner which is often more believable.

Step 3 – Structure Your Presentation

A common technique for trying to calm nervousness is memorizing what you intend to say. But all this does is make your delivery sound like it is coming from a robot. If you miss a word or draw a blank, your whole presentation is thrown off and then your nervousness compounds itself with every remaining second. It is far better to structure your presentation so that you give yourself clues to what is coming next.

- Have a set of key phrases listed on a cue card.
- Refer to these phrases to trigger your mind as to what is coming up next.
- If you're using slides, use these key phrases in your transitions.

This approach helps you control your own uncertainty about whether you will remember what you want to say and the order you want to say it.

Tip

A simple, widely used, and highly effective structure is to tell the audience what you're going to say, then say it, and then recap what you've said. Our article on How to Structure a Presentation covers this in detail.

Step 4 – Practice, Practice, Practice

Although you should avoid memorizing your presentation, you do want to be very comfortable with your delivery. Familiarity brings confidence, and practice helps you to deliver the words naturally. This means they will be coming more from your heart and mind, rather than from a piece of paper.

- Learn the organization and order of your presentation.
- If you do feel the need to memorize, limit it to your opening. This will help you get off to a smooth start.
- Try videotaping yourself. You will see what you look like to others and then you can make a plan to change the things that need changing.
- Use audiotape to listen to how you speak, your tone and your speed, and adjust appropriately.
- Prepare for large speaking events by practicing with a smaller audience first; for example, by inviting colleagues to listen to a dry run during their lunch hour.

Step 5 – Prepare, Prepare, Prepare

Once you know what you are going to say, you need to prepare yourself for the actual delivery.

Decide what you are going to wear – make it comfortable and appropriate.

- Arrive early and get your equipment set up.
- Anticipate problems and have backups and contingencies in place in case something doesn't work, you forget something, etc.
- If possible, give everything one last run through in the real environment.
- Prepare responses to anticipated questions. Try to think like that one person in the front row who always tries to trip the presenter up.

Step 6 – Calm Yourself from the Inside

Nervousness causes physiological reactions which are mostly attributed to the increase of adrenaline in your system. You can counteract these effects with a few simple techniques:

- **Practice deep breathing** – adrenalin causes you to breath shallowly. By breathing deeply your brain will get the oxygen it needs and the slower pace will trick your body into believing you are calmer. It also helps with voice quivers, which can occur when your breathing is irregular.
- **Drink water** – adrenalin can cause a dry mouth, which in turn leads to getting tongue-tied. Have a glass of water handy. Take sips occasionally, especially when you want to emphasize a point.
- **Smile** – this is a natural relaxant that sends positive chemicals through your body.
- **Use visualization techniques** – imagine that you are delivering your presentation to an audience that is interested, enthused, smiling, and reacting positively. Cement this positive image in your mind and recall it right before you are ready to go on.
- Press and massage your forehead to energize the front of the brain and speech center.
- Just before you start talking, pause, make eye contact, and smile. This last moment of peace is very relaxing and gives you time to adjust to being the centre of attention.
- Speak more slowly than you would in a conversation, and leave longer pauses between sentences. This slower pace will calm you down, and it will also make you easier to hear, especially at the back of a large room.
- Move around during your presentation. This will expend some of your nervous energy.

- Stop thinking about yourself. Remember that the audience is there to get some information and it is your job to put it across to them.

Key Points

When it comes to presenting, nerves are inevitable. Letting them get the better of you is not. You need to develop a strategy for taking the focus off your nervousness and putting that energy to positive use. By controlling as much of the uncertainly as you can, you increase your confidence in your ability to deliver an excellent presentation. This confidence then counteracts your nerves and you create a positive cycle for yourself.

Nerves are not your enemy and you don't have to fear public speaking. For your next presentation, be knowledgeable, be well practiced and prepared, try out some physical relaxation techniques. Amaze yourself and impress your audience with your calm and cool delivery of a great presentation.

PLANNING AN EFFECTIVE PRESENTATION

A effective presentation makes the best use of the relationship between the presenter and the audience. It takes full consideration of the audience's needs in order to capturc their interest, develop their understanding, inspire their confidence and achieve the presenter's objectives.

Careful planning is essential.

Seven stages in planning a presentation

Preparation

Many factors affect the design of your presentation. A powerful presenter will acknowledge and address each of the following:

- objectives;
- audience;
- venue;
- remit.

Objectives

Why you are making your presentation? Bear in mind what you want to achieve and what you want your audience to take away with them. Once you have decided upon your objectives, you are in a much better position to make strategic decisions about the design and tone of your presentation. For example, a presentation to a seminar group might require a balanced argument, whereas a charity appeal might require a more creative approach. Ask yourself:

- what do you want your audience to have understood?
- what action do you want your audience to take following your presentation?
- how can you best design your presentation to meet your objectives?

Audience

Your audience will have a variety of different experiences, interests and levels of knowledge. A powerful presenter will need to acknowledge these and prepare for and respond to them accordingly. Ask yourself:

- how much will your audience already know about your topic?
- how can you link new material to things they might already understand?
- will you need to win them over to a particular point of view?

You may not be able to answer these questions for each member of your audience but you should have enough information to ensure that you have targeted your material at the right level for their needs. This might involve avoiding technical jargon or explaining abstract concepts with clear practical examples. If you fail to consider your audience's needs, you will fail to appeal to their interest and imagination.

Venue

Where will you be making your presentation? What will the room be like? What atmosphere will the physical conditions create? A large lecture theatre might create a formal atmosphere. Similarly, a seminar room might create a less formal tone. Ask yourself:

- what kind of atmosphere do you wish to create?
- how might the room arrangement affect your relationship with the audience?
- can you do anything to change the arrangement of the room to suit your
- objectives?
- what audio-visual aids can you use?

Remit

You may well have been given a remit for your presentation; you will need to stick to this. For example, you may have been asked to present a paper at a conference in a certain style or meet certain assessment criteria on your course. Ask yourself:

- how much time have you been allocated?
- are you required to stick to a common format or style?
- have any guidelines been set regarding the content of your presentation (i.e. a predetermined title, or a fixed number of overhead transparencies)?

Choosing your main points

Once you have thought about the design of your presentation, you can define your main points. Try presenting no more than three main points in a ten minute presentation. Always allow time for an adequate introduction and conclusion. It is difficult for an audience to follow a more complex argument without significant help from the presenter. A powerful presentation delivers information in a logical, structured manner, building on the previous point and avoiding large jumps in sequence. Ask yourself:

- what are the main points you wish to make?
- are these points structured in a logical, coherent way?
- do these main points reflect your own objectives and take account of the needs of your audience?

Choosing your supporting information

The supporting information helps your audience understand, believe in and agree with your main points. This evidence might take the form of factual data, points of detail or an explanation of process. It might be presented in imaginative ways using diagrams, pictures or video segments. Think about:

- what will add clarity to your argument (explaining complex terms, reminding your audience of any supporting theories)?
- what will add authority to your argument (making connections with other
- people's work, quoting experts, offering evidence from your own research)?
- what will add colour to your argument (showing a video clip or a slide, using a practical example or a vibrant analogy)?

Establishing linking statements

The next stage is to develop the linear flow of your presentation. This can be achieved by using linking statements to show clearly how your main points fit together. Common linking statements include:

- "The next stage in our project was to ...";
- "Another important issue of consideration was ...";
- "By following this argument we can now see that ...".

Linking statements send signals to your audience, highlighting the next point in your argument, linking to earlier ideas or clarifying the stage you have reached in your argument overall. This may be of particular importance in a lengthy presentation where even the most effective presenter has to work hard to keep an audience involved.

Developing an opening

The introduction to your presentation is crucial. It is your first point of contact with your audience; you can either capture or lose your audience's interest in a matter of seconds. Use your introduction to lay a clear foundation for the presentation to follow. Try using the following structure:

- introduce yourself;
- state what you will be talking about (a title or subject area);
- state how you will be talking about it (e.g. by comparing test results or reviewing the supporting literature);
- state what you intend to be the outcome of your presentation (an informed group, a lively discussion);
- state what you expect your audience to do (listen, take notes, read a handout, ask questions before/during/after).

Always give your audience a moment to absorb this information before moving into your first main point.

Developing a conclusion

Your conclusion is another important stage in your presentation. You can use it to remind your audience of your main points, draw these points to a stimulating conclusion and leave your audience with a lasting impression of the quality of your presentation. The following structure provides a powerful conclusion:

- a review of your title or subject area

  "In this presentation I wanted to explore the relationship between X and Y.";

- a summary of your main points

  "We have discussed the following points…";
- a summary of the process you have been through

  "By looking at X we have found that Y …";
- a conclusion clearly drawn from your main points (this must be supported by the detail of your presentation)

  "It is clear that there can be no substantive relationship between X and Y";
- a parting statement to stimulate your audience's thoughts (this might be a question or a bold comment).

Reviewing your presentation

Once you have written your presentation make sure that you review its content. Ask yourself:

- does the presentation meet your objectives?
- is it logically structured?
- have you targeted the material at the right level for your audience?
- is the presentation too long or too short?

DELIVERING AN EFFECTIVE PRESENTATION

An effective presenter needs to be flexible, energetic and enthusiastic. This guide will help you turn your written presentation into an imaginative public performance.

Presentation as performance

Making a presentation puts you on public display. An audience not only listens to your ideas, it also responds to the way you use your voice and your body. You need more than a well written presentation to make an impact. You will also need to deliver it in a lively, flexible and interesting way. In this leaflet we suggest many ideas for invoking energy in your presentation style.

To begin with, imagine that you are in the audience for your presentation. What might:

- grab your attention?
- stimulate your imagination?
- inspire your confidence?
- develop your understanding?

Now think about ways to encourage these things.

Six steps to becoming an effective presenter

Practise

The more familiar you are with your material the more you will be able to inspire your audience's trust and confidence. Do more than practise reading through your material to yourself. If possible, stand up in a room and deliver your presentation to the walls. Get used to hearing your own voice filling a room. Familiarise yourself with the words and phrases in your presentation. Play around with different volumes and see how well you can hear your own voice. Above all, familiarise yourself with the main thrust of your argument and explore how the individual elements of your presentation piece together. This will help you to keep to your chosen objectives and avoid distractions when it comes to your actual delivery.

To read or to learn?

Should you read out your presentation from detailed notes or present it completely from memory? Find a way to compromise between these two approaches. There are dangers in each.

Reading

Reading tends to focus your thoughts on your notes, thus losing contact with your audience. Reading can also reduce your voice to a monotone, removing energy and enthusiasm from your delivery. Directly addressing your audience is much more engaging.

Learning

Learning is fine until you lose your way; for example, a member of the audience asks a question or your overhead projector bulb blows. Always have some form of notes to keep you on the right track. Also, if you over learn your notes you might lose a sense of energy and enthusiasm. Always work for a sense of confident spontaneity.

Find a way of making notes to support your presentation style. The most common form of note making is to use index cards. These can be read at a glance. Use them as visual prompts to guide you through your presentation. Use one card for each main idea, including details of the supporting information for each point. Connect your cards together with a tag or a piece of string so that they can't get out of order.

Assert yourself

An effective presenter needs to be assertive, not aggressive. There are two important Ps.

Posture

It is important to appear confident at all times. Different postures create different moods. A very formal, upright and still posture will create a very different atmosphere from a relaxed and active one. Remember to match your physical behaviour to the objectives underpinning your presentation. If you want to be either formal or informal, make deliberate choices about your physical style and stick to these.

Presence

Have the confidence to fill your space in front of an audience. Avoid apologising for your presence by saying "sorry" (although you must be polite if circumstances so demand - e.g. the session is running over time, or the microphone has stopped working). Also, avoid physical apologies by hiding behind a desk or lectern. You must be confident that the audience wants to listen and that you have something interesting to tell them. Don't be afraid to wait for an audience to settle down before you start speaking or to ask for quiet if this does not happen.

Make contact with your audience

One of the key challenges faced by the presenter is to establish links with her/his audience (a poor presenter appears to be speaking to an empty room). Making contact helps to maintain an audience's interest and encourages them to believe that you are genuinely interested in talking to them. You can make contact with your audience in a number of ways, including:

- eye contact;
- gestures;
- spoken contact;
- your use of language.

Eye contact

Eye contact is part of everyday communication and an audience can feel uncomfortable if they are denied it. Making eye contact with individuals gives them a sense of involvement in your presentation and helps to convey your objectives on a personal level. Make sure that you share eye contact with all members of a small audience and all areas of a large audience. Regularly shift your focus around the room, not so that you look nervous, but to help involve as many people as possible in your talk.

A handy tip: if you can't make eye contact in a large group, don't look at the floor or ceiling (this looks like boredom or rudeness). Try looking at people's foreheads. The people sat around them will read this as eye contact even if the individual won't.

Gesture

People use their arms and hands in every day conversation to add emphasis or to help describe events. Presenters will therefore look rather awkward if they keep their hands in their pockets or rooted firmly at their sides. Use gestures to welcome your audience, to add emphasis to your main points or to indicate an ending. Try to use open gestures which move away from your body, extending them out to your audience. This helps to break any audience/presenter divisions. Make sure that all gestures are controlled and precise; too much movement will appear nervous and unfocussed. Always watch against distracting your audience from the content of your presentation. You should continually be trying to find ways to help them listen and understand.

Spoken contact

Acknowledge your audience by making verbal contact with them. At the beginning of your talk ask if they can see and hear you, or check that lighting and sound levels on audio-visual equipment are satisfactory. During your presentation, ask rhetorical questions that you can then answer (e.g. "How do we know this was true?" or "So, what does this prove?"). At the end of your talk give the audience an opportunity to ask questions or to clarify detail— this encourages them to take ownership of your material.

The use of questions is an important tool. Questions involve your audience's mind in a more stimulating way than simply asking them to sit and listen to your talk. Draw an audience in with clear, focused questions.

Language

Your use of language is particularly important in developing and sustaining a relationship with your audience. Try using language that involves your audience. For example, asking questions such as "What can we learn from this?" or "How did we arrive at this conclusion?" involves your audience in an exploratory process or discussion. When looking at visual aids, introduce them by saying "If we look at this slide we can see that .." or "This slide shows us that…". Use language that is welcoming and involving throughout your presentation.

Use your voice

Your voice is a very flexible and powerful tool. You can use it in many different ways by varying the:

- volume;
- pace and
- pitch.

Volume

Make sure that your voice is loud enough for your audience to hear clearly. Speaking too loudly or too quietly can make it difficult for your audience to follow your presentation. Listen to people speaking in normal conversation. They tend to raise or lower their volume for emphasis. For example, they may speak loudly when giving an instruction but softly when apologising. To add energy to your presentation, use these colourful changes to your best advantage: a conspiratorial whisper can draw an audience in; a loudly spoken exclamation can make them sit up and listen.

Pace

Make sure that the speed of your delivery is easy to follow. If you speak too quickly or too slowly your audience will have difficulty following your talk. To add life to your presentation, try changing the pace of your delivery. A slightly faster section might convey enthusiasm. A slightly slower one might add emphasis or caution.

Pitch

The pitch of your voice also varies in day to day conversation and it is important to play on this when making a presentation. For example, your pitch will raise when asking a question; it will lower when you wish to sound severe.

Play around with the volume, pace and pitch of your voice when practising your presentation. Find different ways of saying the same sentence. Explore different ways of adding emphasis to your main points. Always try to convey enthusiasm and energy through your use of your voice.

Breathe

Always remember to breath steadily and deeply. If you are anxious about making a presentation your breathing will become fast and shallow. This will affect the quality of your voice and your ability to speak clearly for extended periods of time. Try to take a few deep breaths before you make your presentation, making a conscious effort to slow your breathing down and taking in more air with each breath. During your presentation, use pauses after questions or at the end of sections to allow comfortable breathing patterns. Don't be afraid to slow down the pace of your presentation if your breathing becomes uncomfortable.

Drink

It is a good idea to have some liquid to hand to quench your thirst if you are speaking for a long time. However, be careful not to gulp ice-cold water before you go on as this constricts your throat and affects the quality of your voice. Drink a warm (not hot) cup of tea to relax your throat and ease your speaking voice.

And finally ... a note about humour

Only use humour if you know it will work. Humour needs to be relaxed and confident - if used badly, it will only heighten senses of awkwardness and anxiety if these are already present. Use humour if you know you can and if you feel it is appropriate to do so.

Conclusion

Continually explore your personal style using any or all of the above suggestions in different combinations for different effects. Above all, remember two main points:

- be yourself— even in the most formal of surroundings you will need to be yourself. No one will be impressed if you try to perform like a classical actor or act like a stand-up comedian;
- avoid any behaviour that might be off-putting to your audience— always be deliberate and clear in your use of your voice and physical actions.

The next study guide in this series, Using visual aids, looks at how you can use visual images to increase the impact of your presentation.

CHAPTER 18

Stress Management

This chapter aims to help you recognise and understand anxiety and nervousness which may arise during presentations or interviews. This is sometimes referred to as performance anxiety. The guide also offers strategies to help you minimise any detrimental effects and provides details for a number of further sources of help and advice.

PERFORMANCE ANXIETY?

Many people feel nervous when speaking publicly, either to a room of course peers, conference delegates or an interview panel. This is sometimes referred to as performance anxiety.

Performance anxiety, however, is not necessarily harmful; a slightly increased anxiety level can motivate you to do the work needed so that you are effectively prepared for the event: it can make you more alert and energised. However, should your anxiety levels and nerves become too great, difficulties can occur, which may impair your ability to prepare effectively for and perform during the event.

WHAT CAUSES IT?

Performance anxiety and nerves can be caused by many factors which may include:

- worrying about past performance during presentations or interviews;
- how you will compare with your friends or other students;
- any negative consequences if you don't do as well as you would like;
- the reaction of others to your work.

Lack of preparation as indicated by:

- hurriedly writing the presentation at the last minute;
- not rehearsing and practising your speech;
- not thinking in advance about the kinds of questions the interviewer might ask.

You may not be able to identify a particular cause, you may just be aware that you typically experience nerves or anxiety at the prospect of a presentation or interview.

WHAT HAPPENS WHEN YOU ARE NERVOUS?

When you experience nerves, anxiety or stress about an event, certain physical reactions happen automatically. If you recall a time when you were interviewed or made a presentation you may have noticed that you reacted in some of the following ways:

- your voice trembled;
- you had sweaty palms;
- you experienced shortness of breath;
- your heartbeat accelerated;
- you had butterflies or an upset stomach;
- you experienced a generalised feeling of fear.

These reactions are driven by the production of hormones and equip us to fight or escape from situations that are dangerous or threatening. This is known as the fight or flight response; your body is alert, ready for action and is preparing itself to cope with the situation. Once the threatening event is over, your body will gradually return to normal. Although this process is designed to assist you during potentially threatening situations, it can cause difficulties, particularly if your level of anxiety is too great and/or it occurs for a long time period.

WHAT ARE THE SIGNS OF PERFORMANCE ANXIETY?

There is a range of signs which may indicate that you are experiencing performance anxiety and these signs could begin just before your presentation or interview, hours or days before it, or even at the moment you find out about it. Signs can even persist throughout your presentation or interview.

The signs could include negative thoughts such as 'I'll never manage it'; 'It will be a disaster'; 'I'm no good at this'. Having thoughts of this kind can distort your perception of the event and create a cycle whereby the more negatively you think about it, the more stressed and anxious you become, which in turn can increase your negative thoughts about it and so on.

Holding negative thoughts can also have a big impact on your feelings; you may be aware of feeling scared about the event or you may feel generally irritable but not be sure why. You may also observe behavioural changes, such as putting off thinking about and planning for the presentation or interview, or alternatively being unable to stop thinking about and planning for it. You may also experience physical changes, such as experiencing headaches, changes in your appetite or developing sleeping difficulties.

STRATEGIES TO HELP YOU DEAL WITH PERFORMANCE ANXIETY

The strategies outlined below offer some simple steps that you can take to try to control your level of performance anxiety. However, for them to be effective you need to be active in implementing them prior to and during the event.

Develop positive thinking and visualisation skills

As described previously, having negative thoughts is one indicator that you may be experiencing performance anxiety. It is useful, therefore, to be aware of some of the common negative thought patterns so that you can try to replace them with positive thoughts.

Negative thought	Positive replacement
'It will be a disaster.'	'I will aim to do the best I can.'
'I never do any good at this kind of thing, it's bound to go horribly wrong.'	'Just because I had a problem with this is in the past does not mean that things are bound to go wrong.'
'They won't like me.'	'They like what they have read on my application form/CV otherwise they would not be interviewing me.'
'They are looking for ways of catching me out.'	'They are giving me an opportunity to demonstrate my knowledge of something that I have worked hard to understand.'
'They will ask me about an item on my application form that is a weakness of mine.'	'If it had been a big problem they would not have short listed me for interview. How can I talk about it in the most positive way?'
'I will fail my degree and never get the career of my choice if I don't do well in this presentation.'	'The marks for this presentation are only a small percentage of my overall degree. If I don't do as well as I would like there will be other opportunities to improve my marks.'

Try to become aware if you are having negative thoughts and, if so, think of a positive replacement for them (you could consider asking your friends to help you with this).

It may also be useful to visualise yourself successfully completing the task. Imagine yourself coming out of the interview or presentation and moving on to other things in your life beyond the anxiety provoking experience. Plan a treat or social event afterwards that is not dependent upon the outcome.

Using these processes will help you to keep a sense of perspective about the event and stop things from spiralling out of control. Focus on the present and what you can do now to deal with the situation, rather than dwelling on what you should have done or how similar events went in the past.

PLAN AND PRACTISE YOUR PRESENTATION CAREFULLY

Planning and practising for your presentation or interview carefully can have a number of beneficial effects on your anxiety levels, including helping you to feel more confident and in control prior to the event. The better prepared you are and the more you know your material, the more likely you will be to recall it when you are feeling nervous or stressed.

When you are rehearsing for your interview or presentation, picture yourself as if you are in front of your audience/interview panel and rehearse out loud. If possible, do this in front of some friends who could give you constructive feedback about your verbal and non-verbal communication, and your time-keeping. If you do not want a friend to watch you, consider making an audio or video tape of yourself. You can then listen or watch the tape and provide your own feedback. Identify at least five positive things about your skills, as well as areas for further development.

Preparing for questions at the end of a presentation or during an interview may also help to lower your anxiety levels. Read over your presentation notes or application form critically to identify areas of possible weakness and prepare positive answers. Friends and staff in the University may be able to assist with this. During the event, give yourself time to think of a response to the question by pausing, repeating the words of the question or, if you need longer, asking for a few moments to consider your answer.

Practical advice and guidance on how to prepare and deliver powerful presentations is available from the Student Learning Centre, College House. A range of free study guides is available and there are Individual Consultations for one-to-one advice. For guidance on interview technique, the Careers Service offers a range of guides, videos, one-to-one consultations and workshops.

MAP OUT YOUR ANXIETIES

You may find it helpful to identify the aspects of the situation which are causing you the greatest levels of anxiety, in order to plan steps to prevent them from becoming a reality. Imagine the presentation or interview and write down the aspects which cause you to feel particularly anxious, and then identify something you could do in advance which would help to prevent this from occurring. For instance, if you are worried about using equipment, make sure that you practise using it before the event. Alternatively, if you are worried that a weakness will be highlighted, plan a positive response to this in advance.

LOOK AFTER YOURSELF

Taking care of yourself physically and emotionally will help to control your anxiety levels by making you feel relaxed and using up some of the nervous energy that is produced when you are under stress. The Student Learning Centre Study Guide: Exam Stress explains the following strategies in more detail and is recommended as a source for further information.

- Eat a well balanced diet which limits alcohol, caffeine and sugary foods.
- Aim to have between six to eight hours sleep per night.
- Exercise regularly as this uses up nervous energy and relaxes muscles.
- Make time for fun such as participating in a sport or hobby.

- Practise taking control of your breathing. Concentrate on breathing out to a slow count of four; the breathing in will take care of itself.

ON THE DAY OF THE EVENT

Expect that you will feel some nerves or anxiety

On the day of the presentation or interview expect that you will have some nerves or anxiety. This is your body's way of preparing itself to cope, so do not try to eliminate your nerves totally, but aim to keep them manageable.

You can also expect to feel nervous particularly at the start of the interview or presentation and it is likely that you may feel shaky or possibly your voice will tremble. If this does happen, change to a slower pace, breathe more deeply and expect that the tremble/ shakiness will go away. People do expect to see some nerves at the outset. Allow yourself time to settle into the presentation or interview and then you can perform to the best of your ability as it continues.

Nerves can make you speed up or slow you down on the day. If you are using note cards in a presentation, you may find it useful to put reminders to yourself to check the time and to think about whether you need to slow down or speed up.

Think positively: don't jump to conclusions about people's reactions

Do not forget to use the positive thinking skills that you have been practising up to the event on the day itself. Tell yourself you can do it and try not to jump to conclusions about how people appear to be reacting to you. Some people may look stern or uninterested, when they are actually just concentrating very hard on what you are saying.

Try to relax yourself physically

Remember to use the breathing exercise that you have practised. You may also find it useful to do a relaxation exercise to release muscular tension in places such as the neck and shoulders. Take some deep breaths, aim to increase the distance between your shoulders and your ears. This will help to lengthen your muscles and relieve tension.

Be careful about what you eat and drink

Avoid food or drink that is high in sugar, alcohol or caffeine as these can make you feel more jittery. Immediately prior to the event it can be better to have a warm rather than cold drink. Cold drinks tend to constrict the vocal chords and may increase the likelihood of your voice trembling.

Prepare strategies in case you feel overwhelmed

Do something that will distract you from the frozen state. You could change your posture or focus your gaze just above peoples' eyes for a few seconds which may help you to collect your thoughts. If you are really stuck you may need to ask for a short amount of time to concentrate because you have lost your train of thought through nerves. People are generally supportive and will think more positively if they see you trying to gain composure.

Reward yourself for a job done

Praise yourself afterwards for a job done no matter how well or badly you think it went, and then do something which you enjoy as a special treat.

WHAT CAN I DO TO SUPPORT A FRIEND WITH PERFORMANCE ANXIETY?

Friends are usually the first people we turn to when we are under stress. Often, very simple things can help.

- Help your friend to keep a sense of perspective about the event and to develop positive thinking about the situation. Encourage them to do the best that they can and to accept that they are not a failure if they do not do as well as they would have liked.

- Help them to rehearse and practise their presentation or interview techniques. Provide them with constructive feedback which highlights some good aspects of their techniques along with identifying areas that could be improved.
- If you will be at the presentation, give your friend some positive encouragement and feedback during the session. Smile, show interest, ask a question.
- Be there to meet them after the presentation or interview and support them no matter how well or badly they think they did.
- Plan something enjoyable to do afterwards to celebrate a job done.
- Encourage them to follow the strategies outlined in the guide and to seek further support if these strategies are not helping.
- Don't take them to the pub beforehand - it rarely has the desired effect!

CHAPTER 19

Nonverbal Communication Training for Hospitality Industry

Most people believe that speech is our main form of communication. In reality, oral communication is a fairly recent development in the history of human evolution. Before speech was developed, humans relied on body language and deep throat sounds to convey attitude, emotions and feelings. Today, nonverbal communication, or paralanguage, which includes body language, facial expressions, the use of personal space and to nation, still makes up approximately 65 percent of our communications, whereas verbal element makes up the remaining 35 percent. While verbal communication is often used to convey facts and data, nonverbal communication expresses our physical, mental, or emotional states.

Anthropologist claims that an average person can recognize approximately 250,000 facial expressions. The authors of "Definitive of Book of Body Language", Allan and Barbara Pease, believe that body language accounts for 60 to 80 percent of the impact made during a business negotiation. In addition, people draw their initial opinion about a person whom they have just met in less than four minutes. Much of this opinion is based on their conscious and subconscious observation of the new person's nonverbal cues. In fact, in our verbal language, we have a number of descriptive vocabularies, which we use to describe certain nonverbal behaviors that many of us intuitively understand. Word phrases such as "a cocky attitude" or "a smirk" elicit mental images of certain body posture and facial expressions. Our paralanguage is such an important part of the human communication process that in a face-to-face situation, what we see means more to us than what we hear. According to Allan and Barbara Pease, non-verbal signals carry about five times as much impact as the oral communication. If what we see and what we hear happen to contradict each other, we, especially women, tend to disregard the verbal content and rely on nonverbal signals. This intuitive understanding of nonverbal behaviors is reflected in one of the old proverbs: "People may doubt what you say. But they never doubt what you do.

Yet, since the development of speech, most people tend to rely on verbal language and are not even aware of that there is another level of communication going on with all of us. Men, in this case, are less aware of the ongoing nonverbal communication between individuals than most women. This could be because women are more in Tune with communication in general and tend to send out more nonverbal cues, such as nodding and eye contact, while carrying on a conversation. Women are also more in Tune with their own emotions as well as the emotions of others.

NONVERBAL COMMUNICATION IS ONGOING AND OFTEN WITHOUT OUR KNOWING

While speech can be turned on or off, allowing us to choose whether to express our thoughts or to keep them to ourselves, nonverbal communication is ongoing. The way we stand, sit, or use our hand gestures and facial expressions, all send out stronger signals than the words we speak. Our body language reveals our feeling, attitude and emotion, even to strangers and often does so without our knowing. For example, when two individuals unconsciously match each other's body gestures, called "matching and mirroring", it clearly indicates that they feel that they are on the same wavelength with each other. It also implies that they have developed certain trust and goodwill. Further, when people are at the 'making friends' stage, they tend to mirror each other's gestures in a subconscious effort to reach out. Conversely, many people instinctively know that when the conversation with another person is not going well. If two people mismatch their body gestures, we know that trust has not yet been established and perhaps, there might be disagreements between them. In addition, if one shows hand gestures such as touching the ear, eyes or back of the head (especially among men), the message is that disinterest has set in and that he/she is ready to move on.

HOTEL INDUSTRY NEEDS TO EMPHASIZE NONVERBAL COMMUNICATION TRAINING

More and more, the service industry begins to realize that in order to offer the best customer service, company-wide customer care training is important. However, much of the training involves verbal behaviors. For example, one time I flew with one of the American airline companies. It was obvious that the ground staff was trained to address each passenger by his/her name. Even though they addressed me by my name, which supposedly signaled friendliness and caring, their nonverbal communication said something else. To begin with, there was no eye contact. Also, some of them addressed my name while their shoulders were turned away or their head was facing a different direction. This made their verbal communication seem insincere and half hazard. Under these circumstances, most of us would trust the accuracy of nonverbal cues rather than verbal behaviors. The airline company simply neglected to train the ground crew members, so that they understand that:

- a message is not properly communicated unless it is understood and agreed upon by the receiver;
- in order to be credible, both verbal and nonverbal messages must be consistent.

In business, any top sales executive or contract negotiator could testify on the importance of understanding their clients' or opponents' paralanguage. After all, hotel business is people business. People communicate - verbally and nonverbally. It is only natural that hotel staff should acquire a good understanding of nonverbal communication and be able to identify their guests' emotional state as well as their likes and dislikes. Not only that, hotel staff should be able to use nonverbal communication to convey friendliness, helpfulness and genuine warmth. They should also learn to eliminate negative paralanguage that may send out the wrong message. For example, matching and mirroring can be used to send strong positive signals while subconsciously assuring the guests that the hotel staff likes them and agrees with what they are saying. This will instantly create a positive and harmonious guest relation. On the other hand, a stiff upper lip and cold eyes convey hostility regardless of what one says.

Like the airline company training, much of the hotel guest service training focuses on verbal behaviors. Nonverbal behavior training is not always adequately addressed or properly understood. Perhaps, nonverbal communication training should include more than just smiling, nodding and a few simple and basic gestures. For instance, men and women "mirror" differently. Wrong approach will not achieve the positive result expected and may even cause misunderstanding. Every day we respond to thousands of nonverbal cues and behaviors, that include our facial expressions, handshakes, gestures, tone of our voice, and even our appearance. Nonverbal details reveal who we are and how we relate to other people. Consequently, nonverbal behavior training must be more in depth and broader in scope. After all, nonverbal communication is humans' original language! Hotels that are able to master nonverbal communication will surely establish memorable and long-lasting guest relations.

BENEFITS OF EFFECTIVE COMMUNICATION IN THE HOTEL INDUSTRY

What do you think should be the most important quality of a hotel manager? If someone were to ask me, I'd say it would be the capability to communicate effectively with the staff, colleagues and guests. In this new age of electronic communication, one should not forget that effective verbal and non-verbal communication skills should be emphasized and well-executed in the hospitality industry.

Compelling communication skills are important in a hotel regardless of some staff members not being guest-facing. A few hotels spend considerable amount of money on training their staff to interact with the guests. Good communication skills are a learned art and not a natural skill so one should consider training to enhance staff skills. Excellent communication skills enhance guest experience as it conveys that you are listening to your guests, valuing their feedback and conveying clear messages. Apart from communicating with the guests, your staff ought to know how to write emails. Good communication skills will impress your guests which will further prove beneficial to your hotel business.

Not only does the staff need to communicate successfully with the guests but also with other department employees. Few of the staff members might be able to speak in manageable English but those who don't have English as their first language suffer due to their inability and fail to understand simple instructions and information. Department heads often face problems such as:

- Failing to communicate well with guests which may result in lack of confidence among the staff members
- Failing to process written documents such as emails, reports and other collaterals
- Failing to understand the hotel management software hotels use these days

Being the department head, if you are often facing such challenges then there is a problem and you need to look into it sooner. Here are some suggestions:

CONDUCT STAFF TRAINING

Arrange for a communication skills program that will be helpful for your employees to communicate effectively with the guests in crucial circumstances like dealing with complaints, co-ordinating between departments, attending to guests at the front desk and helping in documentation like menus, bills, reports and other hotel procedures. The training should be conducted once a month so that they get a chance to improve their communication skills. Also, encourage your hotel staff to communicate with each other in English.

LISTEN TO YOUR EMPLOYEES

Successful communication is a two-way process which requires the management to periodically listen to their staff member's views and ideas. If the management head does all the talking, employees tend to become lethargic. You need to listen to your employees as they are the ones dealing with the guests on a direct, day-to-day basis. For all you know, they might have ideas to better customer service or improvising of hotel functions if they encounter problems. The best way to listen to your employees is to hold feedback sessions on a weekly basis, take their inputs seriously and reward them. Motivate your hotel staff to help you in taking the hotel business forward.

TRAIN YOUR STAFF ON ATTENDING TO GUESTS

Your employees should know how to communicate well with your guests. There may be instances where your hotel might receive a complaint from guests in verbal or written form through reviews. The person in-charge to solve these matters must be well-trained in order to handle the issue wisely and subtly rather than ignoring it or dismissing it. Urgent matters can be handled with ease if your staff has good communication and behavioral skills.

THE MIRROR TECHNIQUE

The best way to successful communication is to observe your guest's own communication style and to respond accordingly. For instance, when you are dealing with a guest, you may notice that some guests make small conversations and others may be interested in the issue to be dealt with quickly and spontaneously. So observe your guests and act accordingly as it is important to think how you address your guest or deal with complaints (use humor for light-hearted guests).

RESULTS OF GREAT COMMUNICATION SKILLS

- Improved customer service
- Better understanding of the instructions from supervisors among the staff members
- Great understanding of the latest technology used by hotels
- Boosted confidence to approach guests
- Positive attitude towards the workplace and higher level of understanding between the department heads

As stated above, effective communication skills is a learned art and not a natural skill so it doesn't mean that the relevant skills cannot be developed. Hotels should emphasize on providing communication skills training courses which cover everything from basic communication techniques to advanced empathy skills program.

CHAPTER 20

Skill Development - Concerns and Opportunities

Tourism and Hospitality in India seems a robust growth. With the boom in tourism and hospitality, the trade has adopted multipronged approaches to sustain this growth. There is also focused emphasis for product development and strengthening tourism and hospitality infrastructure. To sustain the hanging demand of the new generation tourists, priority should be given to redesign the experience of the tourists through greater organization and provision of civic facilities, incrcased emphasis on branding and focused marketing of tourism and hospitality products, positioning specially India as a high value destination in new markets.

Over the past few decades, the Indian Diaspora has formed a significant portion of immigrant populations in western countries such as United States and Canada. With a win though, it sought to be the most professional opportunity for qualified Indians; internal customers. Technically the geographical migration of labor from one country to another is known as the brain drain. They take with them the skills and knowledge that they have acquired in their home country. Draining their services contributing towards the development of the country; that promises a far higher standard of living in return for their skills.

To accelerate the development of tourism human capital in the country, the emphasis is laid on Skill development schemes by the Government. The objectives of the scheme are:

I. To provide vocational training to school leavers, existing workers, ITI graduates etc. to improve their employability by optimally utilizing the infrastructure available in Govt., private institutions and the Industry. Existing skills of the persons can also be tested and certified under this scheme.

II. To build capacity in the area of development of competency standards, course curricula, learning material and assessment standards in the country.

We have a difficult group but an interesting one to handle in the Indian Hospitality Industry. The 21st century has witnessed a change in the brain drain pattern wherein the Indian Employers have started to do everything to retain talent. These companies gained the reputation of global hub to absorb India's skilled labor in. Secondly, it is important to work in an environment that offers a tremendous scope of growth at all levels- personal, professional, social and Indian economy. Industry is hopeful for future growth thereby creating employment opportunities for the trained or ready to deliver service staff. Hospitality industry is evolving to newer shores customized to understand the various perspectives of the work force that encounters the competitive challenge with performance management system and customers' satisfaction.

The seasonality of the business has some strategic experiments and results that confuse the management to employ the right number of employees in hotels. This is one of the main reasons why it is the need of the hour as company's responsibility to make sure that the bonafide manpower is aware of what is going on in the firm and do their job. The prescription is the therapy of a complete satiety package of the intrinsic and the extrinsic parameters of the individual delectable organization's composite goal accomplishment, because your work at your work area is of utmost importance - effective and efficient.

"The difference between loyalty and lethargy is productivity". The manpower situation in Indian Hospitality industry suffers high attrition and low on retention. The current supply of skilled trained manpower is estimated to be a very dismal of 8.92 % to the total requirement as per study carried out by Ministry of Tourism. The study anticipates widening gap towards 2016-17. Sources of attrition to be addressed and retention strategies practiced through Customer Satisfaction, Motivation – a means to enhance productivity, Training needs, Married to the job, Understanding customer's righteousness, Festivity enhanced team spirit, Formal customer satisfaction measures, Re-skilling HR through technology, Bridging HR through internal certification courses, Tutoring HR towards customer-oriented approach, Combating stress at the workplace, Internship impetus, Full-time engagement, Encouraging innovativeness, Intra company networking is essential, Decentralization encourages experimentation, Frequent get-togethers of HRD staff and periodic surveys is useful, Process orientation should be strengthened, Entrepreneurship for smaller organizations, Strengthening HRD service sector - Indian Hospitality.

The inconsistency acknowledged; reinventing ourselves becomes an ongoing allure and a standing workittude on our daily things-to-do list. The stipulated work quotient entrusted to us is measurement not of the skill or individual, but the activity output refreshed with a post appraisal slump. Taking the self-assurance, self-assignment, self-assessment test you can draw to the conclusion that you are partly competing with the system through your talented edge towards complete set-up of endeavors and partly making your own domain, or presence in the operational design to enhance the goodwill and brand value along with better industrial health and professional hospitality concern; thereby reduce the chances of attrition understanding trained skilled, semi skilled and to-be-skilled manpower as a resource in a properly executed quality standard to influence public perception, thereby building a Sustainable incredible India.

CHAPTER 21

Body Language of a Front Desk Officer

Front office is the face of the hotel and it has all the responsibility to ensure that all the guest needs are full filed and the request of the guest are taken care off. The better coordination between the guest and the hotel is through Front office the GSS of the guest is always passed through the front office and the guest calls front desk and AYS for any assistance if needed. The front office staffs have the prime responsibility to up sell the rooms and to boost the revenue where possible.

Front desk management is one of the departments of hotel management that manages and handles the meetings, sort mail, answer the phone and fix up appointments top management, maintenance of record and details, data entry and other office communications.

To get your hotel business flourishing you will need a compatible front desk management. Its importance can be measured with the fact that front desk people are the one who welcome the guests and their impressive gestures can impact the future business.

Since the front desk is the face of the hotel and first person to contact for booking and reservations or to meet on the entering of the office, he/she must have a sense of calm and courtesy in

his/her profession. Personal qualities play a vital role in the front desk professional.

Front desk receptionists are responsible for making the best first impression on behalf of her employer. Many types of companies hire front desk receptionists to greet customers and visitors as well and handle lightweight office duties. People who succeed as front desk receptionists like people and are good communicators, and many receptionists use the position as a catalyst to higher paying jobs with more responsibilities.

Step 1

Hone your people skills. As the first line of defense against disgruntled customers, pushy salesmen and important business clients, you will need to be comfortable interacting with many personalities both on the phone and in person. Balance friendliness with professionalism.

Step 2

Learn basic business skills, such as how to use word processing and spreadsheet programs. Your employee may have specialized software he will want you to learn as well as how to operate the telephone system. Be prepared to multitask because you may have people standing in front of you while handling phone calls or clerical work as well. Strive to stay busy with administrative tasks between phone calls and visitors.

Step 3

Dress the part of company ambassador. Clothes should always be cleaned and pressed. Whether the company dress policy is business casual or professional, you should strive to dress as if are preparing for an interview. Avoid clothing that is too tight, too short or too low cut. Your goal is to present a conservative image of confidence and helpfulness.

Step 4

Learn as much about the company as possible. A large part of your job is to direct visitors to the correct department or answers. The more you know about the company the more effectively you can accomplish this task. Spend your spare time honing up on company policies, products and services. Review the company organizational chart and prioritize learning the names and schedules of upper management.

Step 5

Before accepting a front desk receptionist job, ask what specialized skills and requirements are necessary to complete the job. For example, a medical receptionist many need to understand medical billing and basic medical terminology while hotel front desk clerks may spend a lot of time on their feet and be expected to work nights and weekends.

When you speak with someone, you offer some certain things to your listeners two ways: By speaking and by gesturing your body. The person, to whom you speak, gets meaning from you not from your speaking but from your gesturing. This is your body language and the top most important thing to remember that every time you handle something, be serious about your body language. Here are some tips for you to convey to the customer as a front desk officer:

- Speak with your customers or anybody of the hotel with a smiling face. A smiling face says that whatever you are talking about all are truth and you are also realizing the other person's problem and is possible for you to solve his/her problem. The other meaning of your smiling face is all times you try to solve any problem of the customer and you are prepared for helping in any need. It is the best way to convince the customer and to raise your personality by an original smiling face. You should know that a calm and friendly smile of your face will drag the customer to your hotel because your body language welcomes the new comers.

- As everything has its own language; you should be conscious about your dress. Maybe well dress or wrong dress but it has own language to the on-lookers. To get a positive feedback from the people to whom you need to talk, as a front officer, surely should be approach yourself with well dress, I mean a becoming dress. You have to keep in mind that a hotel desk is not your home. So, to be a professional, confident, and engaged desk officer, you have to discover the meaning of the dress you are in.

- Do you consciously shake hands every time and feel the difference of the different people. Hand shaking is an important matter for you. When you shake hands your customers want to get a greeting by feeling your hand shaking. Never shake hands as usual to get a bad feedback from your customers.

- As a body language, eye contact is also a great thing. When you talk to the customer, keep a direct eye contact with smiling face. Never show extra curiosity or conspiracy with eyes. And, never answer the questions of the customer engaging your eyes with other works or keeping to the ground. Keep your eyes natural at the time of asking something or answering something.

- It may be hesitating for you when you are not clear what to do with your arms and hands in front of the customers. Being unusual, people generally try to do anything with their arms or with finger. But, the professional stance is to keep hands at your side as usual. If you don't feel comfortable, then hold papers or something in the excuse of preparing for the next work. Never show down extra business or anger towards the customers.

- Posture your body for the gentle view. It is good for you and for the business. When you are seated on or talking to the customer even walking in the hotel, keep in the mind that customer will follow your posturing.

COMMANDMENTS OF FRONT-DESK CLERKS

First Impressions

As the first person most customers see, front-desk clerks need to represent their companies with professionalism and friendliness. A polished appearance and an obvious willingness to help set the tone for a customer's experience. Greet customers with a smile and immediately ask how you can help.

Honesty

Regardless of the setting, most clerks direct customers to somewhere else — a hairdresser, restaurant table or someone in the company — and there's often a wait. Be honest about wait times, and don't promise what might not be delivered. If you don't know the answer to a question, honestly say so and inform the customer you'll get the information.

Focus

Many things compete for attention at a front desk, from ringing phones to colleagues, but when a customer is in front of you, give her your undivided attention. Focusing solely on a customer's needs gives the impression that customer service is a top company priority.

Body Language

Smile with sincerity at every customer, but also pay attention to your body language, which can send negative signals. Stand straight without slouching, look customers in the eye and don't sigh or roll your eyes at any point. Whether you're sitting or standing, lean slightly forward to indicate attention.

Demeanor

Back up your smile with an outgoing, friendly personality. Being positive and cheerful can often overcome even the most gruff customer. Remain calm at all times, particularly with angry or flustered customers and show sympathy when it's warranted.

Work Area

A clean and organized work area gives a good impression. Provide welcoming touches in your lobby or waiting area, such as flowers and magazines. A reception area is a good place to introduce customers to the business, so keep company brochures, business cards or other materials handy.

Technical Expertise

Master all of the equipment used in the job, from telephone systems to reservation software. These are tools that help you focus on providing efficient service to customers, Learn the basics of your business so you can answer customer questions.

Telephone Etiquette

Answer phones cheerfully and professionally. If your company provides a script, follow it. If you're helping a customer and need to answer the phone, excuse yourself politely, finish as expeditiously as possible and apologize for the interruption.

Personal Service

Learn the names of regular customers and call all of your customers by name, using a title such as Mr. or Mrs. unless asked to do otherwise. Offer little services that exceed expectations to impress customers, such as serving beverages, hanging up coats or recommending a service.

Final Impressions

As the last person some customers may see, acknowledge their visit to leave a lasting final impression. Ask if there's anything else they need, say goodbye and wish them a pleasant day.

FRONT DESK COORDINATOR DUTIES

A front desk coordinator assists customers, patients and clients with registration needs, payments for services and general information requests. Front desk coordinators are often called front desk receptionists or front desk information clerks, and their direct supervisor is typically the office manager. Front desk coordinators work at medical offices, hotels, private businesses, salons, schools, nonprofit organizations, and government agencies to greet clients and perform administrative tasks.

Client, Patient and Customer Needs

Front desk coordinators sit in prominent places in their buildings or offices so they can quickly and conveniently greet and address incoming customers. They might answer customer inquiries, direct patients to waiting rooms or other offices, update customer contact information, and notify departments of arriving customers or patients. Front desk coordinators also answer and direct incoming calls and respond to customers' questions over the phone. Many receive payments for products or services, print receipts, and enter financial transactions in cash registers or computer software programs. They also accept job applications from individuals who fill them out in person and send the applications to appropriate departments.

Administrative Duties

Front desk coordinators perform administrative duties when they are not interacting with customers. They file paperwork, maintain computer files, perform data entry, order inventory, process financial documents, update reservations, sort incoming and outgoing mail, keep appointment calendars, and give messages to staff and management in other parts of the building. Some front desk coordinators supervise lower-level front desk staff and coordinate services with other departments. For example, hotel front desk coordinators often notify cleaning crews, hospitality workers, concierges, bellboys, parking attendants and food services when patrons have specific requests.

Security Services

In some businesses, hospitals, schools and government agencies, front desk coordinators assist with security measures. Even though they don't usually carry weapons or hold security officer credentials, they might ask to see visitors' identification cards or run employee badges through computerized scans. Front desk coordinators might also monitor access to restricted departments to ensure only permitted customers and employees enter. Front desk coordinators often work closely with security personnel to maintain the safety and integrity of operations within their facilities.

Troubleshooting

Front desk coordinators are highly visible, so visitors often approach them for help with problems or concerns. They are the catchall for issues that don't require the assistance of other departments. Front desk coordinators use their problem-solving and troubleshooting skills to assist clients and respond to internal needs. For example, university front desk coordinators help students who lose their room or residence hall keys. Some front desk clerks call locksmiths when customers or clients lock their keys in their cars; assist with lost and found searches; and route personal messages to students, patients and employees. Front desk coordinators call repair and cleaning crews for maintenance needs and contact emergency personnel when necessary.

CHARACTERISTICS OF RECEPTIONIST

Receptionists typically operate the front desk of a business. They answer phones, greet clients, provide directions or information and organize files. A high school diploma and good communication skills are common requirements for the job, according to the U.S. Bureau of Labor Statistics. To excel as a receptionist, you need the right combination of personal traits and professional skills.

Great Listener

While receptionists often play the role of message sender, awesome receptionists are usually great listeners first. In a doctor's office, for example, the receptionist must listen carefully to a caller to get basic information about his symptoms and schedule. In a service business, a great receptionist must quickly determine the needs of individual prospects or clients and then ensure those needs are met as efficiently as possible.

Helpful Attitude

Poor, average and even good receptionists can become burned out by the routine and monotony of answering phones and greeting clients. An awesome receptionist doesn't have this problem. Instead, she has a natural interest in people and a helpful attitude. She doesn't view each phone call or guest as an intrusion, but rather as an opportunity to excel at her job. A highly skilled receptionist at a visitor's information center, for example, will answer calls enthusiastically and provide all of the necessary information to help people plan trips or find their way around.

Patient

Not all patrons or clients are a joy to deal with. An awesome receptionist is patient, flexible and accommodating in dealing with different personality types and communication styles. A hotel receptionist might have to deal with some guests who are especially demanding, surly or unpleasant after a long, tiring trip. Showing patience, listening to concerns with compassion and taking the time to resolve issues are all hallmarks of a high-quality receptionist.

Organized

An awesome receptionist balances her strong interpersonal qualities with effective organizational skills. She must maintain an organized workspace so she can communicate clearly and efficiently with customers, suppliers, associates and supervisors. In a business office, the receptionist often prepares outgoing mail and receives incoming mail. She may also have invoicing and billing responsibilities. To handle these tasks properly, she must have a system in place that lets her access the right information in a timely and accurate manner.

CHAPTER 22

Managing Service Quality in Hospitality Industry Through Nonverbal Communication

Delivering good service to customers is the main goal that every service business strives to accomplish from time to time. The ability for a service provider to deliver quality service is considered an essential strategy for success and survival in today's competition. In this case, service encounter is a critical part of the service delivery process because it gives impact to customer's evaluations of service consumption experiences. Therefore, there have been several studies and researches focusing on service encounter as it is believed that there is a causal relationship between the customer perception of service quality and the service encounter. Service encounter is one of the factors influencing customer perceptions of service quality, satisfaction and value as shown in the Fig 1.

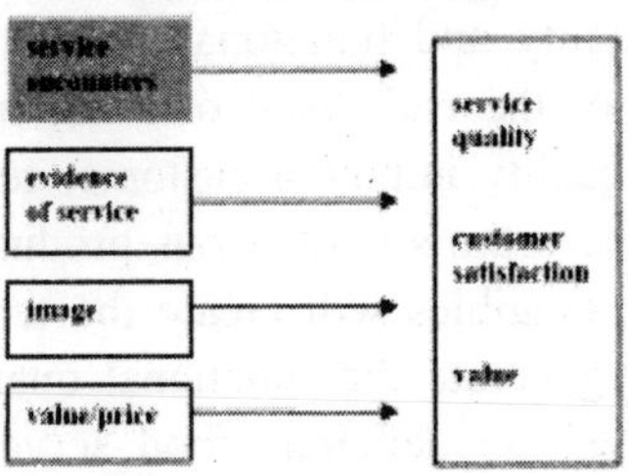

Figure 1. Factors Influencing Customer Perceptions of Service

Hospitality industry is one of the service sector, with relatively high level of customer contact. The higher the level of customer contact the more numerous and longer service encounters between customers and service employees. It implies that more attention must be focused on how to manage all the possible service encounters which will much influence the service quality of the hospitality organization and in the end the profit. Many hospitality organizations have invested considerably to develop service-delivery system which will ensure that customers will receive consistently high-quality service in every service encounter. This makes service encounter or 'moment of truth' in hospitality industry become much more important to be taken care of in the future.

While considerable research has been conducted in the service sector in general focusing on service encounters, specific concern in managing service encounters in hospitality industry has received very little attention. The objectives of this article are to explore from a theoretical perspective how to manage service quality through managing the service encounters that takes place in hospitality industry. It also aims to set a framework of investigation for future empirical research.

SERVICE QUALITY

Service quality is determined by what customers perceive. It means that customers play an important part in judging service quality. Very often companies define service quality apart from what the customers perceive of the quality so that time and money are poorly invested to poor quality programs.Reseacher identified two dimensions in service quality as it is perceived by customers; they are technical quality and functional quality. The technical quality is the outcome or the end result of a service production process. The functional quality is how a customer receives the service and how he experiences the simultaneous production and consumption process. All the tangibles will create the technical quality but the intangibles will generate the functional quality. For example in a restaurant setting, the delicious food served to the guest is the technical quality of a service; while how the guest is treated and served by the waiter is the functional quality. Both of them give influence to the customer in perceiving the service quality. Very often the service provider who performs better in functional quality will gain competitive advantage when most of service providers provide relatively the same technical quality.

Service Quality Dimensions

In evaluating service quality, consumers consider five dimensions:

1. Reliability: ability to perform the promised service dependably and accurately
2. Responsiveness: willingness to help customers and provide prompt service
3. Assurance: employee's knowledge and courtesy and their ability to inspire trust and confidence
4. Empathy: caring, individualized attention given to customers
5. Tangibles: appearance of physical facilities, equipment, personnel, and written materials.

These dimensions are generally considered by consumers when they want to procure a service or when they want to estimate service quality. In the same way, these dimensions are very much contemplated when consumers experience the 'moment of truth'.

SERVICE ENCOUNTER OR "MOMENT OF TRUTH"

The term service encounter and 'moment of truth' are used interchangeably when discussing the period of time where customers interact directly with a service. As it is stated that 'moment of truth' is "a point in service delivery where customers interact with service employees or self-service equipment and the outcome may affect perceptions of service quality". In the 'moment of truth', a careless mistake by an employee, a rude behavior or an unanticipated request by a guest can result in a dissatisfied guest. It is the crucial moment for service provider to influence customer perception of service

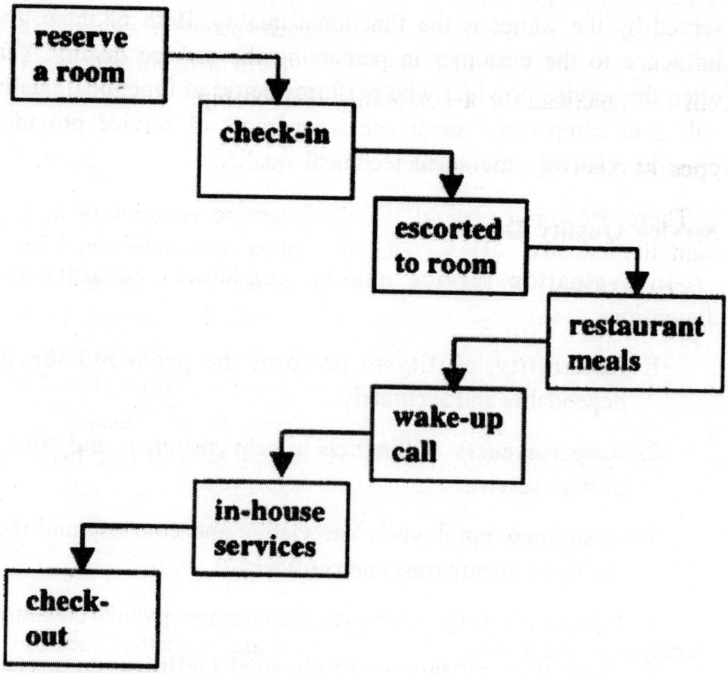

Figure 2. 'Cascade' in 'moments of truth' For a Hotel Visit

quality. For example, a hotel guest may experience several service encounters when booking a room, checking into the hotel, being escorted to a room by a bellman, having meals in the hotel restaurant, requesting a wake-up call, using in-house services, and checking out (see Fig. 2). In these encounters hotel guests receive a picture of the hotel's service quality and each encounter contributes to the hotel guest's overall satisfaction and willingness to do business with the hotel organization again. As for the hotel, each encounter is an opportunity to deliver quality service to guests.

Positive service encounters will add up to a shared image of high service quality, whereas the negative ones will give the opposite effect. Hence, a combination of positive and negative encounters will make the customer "feel unsure of the organization's service quality, doubtful of its consistency in service *delivery, and vulnerable to the appeals of competitors*". Besides, each encounter with different people and departments in an organization will also add to or detract from the potential for a continuing relationship.

Types of Service Encounters

There are three general types of service encounters in the hospitality industry: *remote encounters,* phone encounters, and face-to-face encounters. Remote encounters can occur without any direct human contact, such as: booking a room via the Internet. In this case the technical quality is the only point to control as there is no direct interaction with the service provider. While the phone encounter is the type of encounter between an end customer and the organization which occurs over the telephone, such as: booking a room or a table via telephone. In this case, tone of voice, employee knowledge, and effectiveness/efficiency in handling customer issues become important criteria for judging service quality.

As for face-to-face encounters, there is a direct contact between an employee and a customer. Both verbal and nonverbal behaviors are important determinants of service quality as well as the tangible cues such as employee attire, equipment, physical setting and other tangible symbols.

Analysis of Problems and Challenges in Managing Service Encounters

In order to avoid negative service encounters but ensure positive service encounters are in place, it is necessary to find out what sort of things may bring customer satisfaction and what other sort of things may cause customer dissatisfaction in a service encounter.

First of all, there are four common themes identified as the sources of customer satisfaction/ dissatisfaction in memorable service encounters:

1. **Recovery**: employee response to service delivery system failures

2. **Adaptability**: employee response to customer needs and requests
3. **Spontaneity**: unprompted and unsolicited employee action
4. **Coping**: employee response to problem customers

Failure to respond to the four themes accordingly will result in customer dissatisfaction. Therefore, understanding general service behavior is important to anticipate as much as possible the positive service encounters instead of the negative ones.

Secondly, the intangibility characteristic of service becomes another problem because research has shown that customer expectations are higher for services that are more intangible than for services with more tangible features. It becomes a challenge for a hotel organization to add more tangibility in the service encounter that may lessen the chance of a larger gap between customer expectations and perceptions when a problem arises with that encounter. In this manner, the service provider can add more tangibility when delivering the service by showing directly the service process to the customer. For example: in a restaurant setting, the service provider can present directly the food preparation and cooking process to the guests so that they may experiencc the process by themselves and see how the food is prepared. By adding more tangibility to the service we provide, it is more unlikely for a customer to judge a service delivery that so much deviates from the expected service quality. As a result, the service provider will be able to prevent customer dissatisfaction from occurring or at least minimize it so that service quality will be better accomplished.

Thirdly, another point of consideration should also be given to non-verbal communication when managing service encounters. It is commonly known that employee's display of affective characteristics such as "friendliness, responsiveness, and enthusiasm positively influences customer's overall evaluation of service encounter and perceptions of service quality". Moreover, researchers add that both "verbal and non-verbal elements of communication between the service provider and the customer influence customer's affect or subjective feelings, which in turn influence their evaluation of the service encounter". There are several non-verbal cues influencing service encounters, they are:

1. **Kinesics** – body movements such as eye contact, nodding, hand shaking, smiling and adopting a relaxed and open posture;
2. **Paralanguage** – vocal pitch, vocal loudness or amplitude, pitch variation, pauses and fluency;
3. **Proxemics** – the distance and relative postures of the service provider and customer, and particularly the use of touch; and
4. Physical appearance.

When service employees know exactly what are expected from them in terms of non-verbal behavior besides the verbal communication, they will be able to enhance their effective communication skill verbally and non-verbally. As the effective communication skill increases, the service encounter or 'moment of truth' will more positive and the perceived service quality will be enhanced as the five dimensions of service quality are met accordingly.

Nevertheless, it needs some endeavor from the hospitality managers to build the service employee awareness of the importance of non-verbal behavior besides verbal communication in attaining effective communication skill that will enhance service quality. Researchers suggest that in order to make service employee more sensitive to nonverbal cues, the managers can utilize *role-playing* and show *videotapes* of actual service delivery which demonstrate both the positive and negative nonverbal cues. Continuous feedback will also be useful to remind service employees of the importance of non-verbal communication. Periodic surveys, in addition, are important to assess customers' perceptions of service employees' non-verbal behaviour.

Providing incentives can be desirable to encourage service employees to implement the recommended changes in non-verbal behaviour. Thirdly, culture and purchase motivation become two other points to consider when attempting to manage service encounters. The involvement of people in service delivery implies that cultural diversities and norms quickly come into play when customers evaluate service encounters. This is obviously relevant especially in the hospitality industry where there is so much cultural exposure either with the international guests or among the service employees themselves.

The Asians and the Westerners are two different groups of people who have very different cultural backgrounds. Researcher states that Western customers care more about efficiency and timesaving of a service whereas Asian customers emphasizes on the quality of interpersonal relationship between employee and customer. Therefore, service styles in Asia are more people-oriented than in the West, where the efficiency of the service delivery is highly valued. Another thing that differentiates the two groups in terms of service expectation is that the Asians tend to expect the service employees who are lower in social status to provide customers with high levels of service because their culture is characterized by relatively large power distance that reflect social hierarchies. On the other hand, the Western customers tend to expect more classless or democratic service as their culture less accepts of status differences.

Nevertheless, when these two different groups of culture are opposed to purchase motivation, the expectation will be different. For business customers regardless of cultural background, they tend to focus on the output not the style of the service delivery. They are more interested in efficiency (including the speed of service) than in the functional quality of the interaction. Business customers driven by the need for efficiency might focus on the "service outcome" rather than on the "feelings" generated by the service encounter. Leisure customers, in contrast, tend to be more heterogeneous in their expectations according to their cultural background. Asian leisure customers tend to prefer "high-context communication" in which non-verbal cues are more important than explicit expressions. Asian leisure customers expect to be treated as "deserving of high-quality service". Likewise, some non-verbal cues may vary from culture to culture. Eye contact, for example, is very much expected by the Americans whereas in many Oriental cultures it is not proper to look in the eye too often someone who is superior. In fact, a bowed head represents a signal of respect to an authority figure.

Consequently, it is essential for hospitality organizations to develop employee training programs for guest-contact employees, such as: the Front desk employees in the hotel industry, to ensure that they are able to deliver the service the 'right' way. As for the organizations that expect to cater International guests, they need to give the employees a multicultural training program which includes a language training program and cross-cultural understanding to meet the possible cultural expectations of their foreign guests. This idea is in line with a research finding signifying that Front desk employees' performance is critical to guests' baseline evaluation of a hotel's service quality. As for the restaurant, the waiters or waitresses should be trained well so that they will be more aware of how to be able to serve better according to what is expected by the guests and to have more control over the 'moment of truth'.

SERVICE BLUEPRINTS

Service blueprints are pictures or maps of service processes that permit the people involved in designing, providing, managing, and using the service to better understand them and deal with them objectively. A service blueprint simultaneously depicts the service process and the roles of consumers, service providers, and supporting services.

Blueprints are designed by identifying and mapping a process from the consumer's point of view, mapping employee actions and support activities, and adding visible evidence of service at each consumer action step. Key components of service blueprints are consumer actions, "onstage" and "backstage" employee actions, and support processes. Service blueprint accentuates the customer interactions in the service operations processes and, that the line of visibility separated activities of the front stage, where customers obtained tangible evidence of the service, from the back office processing, which was out of customer view. Hence, the service blueprint can facilitate problem solving and create thinking by identifying potential points of failure and highlighting opportunities to enhance customers' perceptions of the service.

ANALYSIS OF THE SERVICE ENCOUNTERS

There are basically nine kinds of service encounters that happen in the service blueprint above as there are interactions between the service employee and the guest. First of all, when the guest calls the restaurant and books a table, there is a telephone interaction between the guest and the service employee who picks up the telephone. This is the first encounter or 'moment of truth' in which the guest will judge the service quality by evaluating the words spoken by the restaurant employee as well as the tone of voice or the non-verbal cues, in this case, the "paralanguage". In this 'moment of truth', it is very important that the service employee speaks the 'right' words in the 'right' way so that the guest will a first good impression about the service quality of the restaurant in his mind and he would want to go on to the next service encounter.

In this encounter, the guest will judge the service quality whether it is courteous, friendly, credible, competent and empathetic or not at all. Very often restaurants fail to attend to this very first encounter in the 'right' way. They fail to instill a good impression or even an excellent one about the service quality in the first place. This can happen since there is a different perception between the guest and the restaurant employee as the service provider on the "point of activation" when the first action in the service encounter begins. It often happens that the service provider perceives that the first action in the service encounter starts when the guest actually arrives and enters the restaurant whereas the guest evaluates the first service encounter at the very first moment he or she contacts the restaurant and has the conversation with a restaurant employee. This can be a critical point in the 'moment of truth' in which the service provider needs to take care.

Secondly, when the guest arrives at the restaurant and he is greeted by a greeter who then asks for the reservation. This leads to the second interaction between the guest and the service employee but this time, it is more than just verbal communication but also non-verbal communication as there is direct contact between the two. When greeting the guest, it is important for the service employee to also demonstrate the 'right' non-verbal cues besides the verbal and tangible cues since all those cues will compose the overall notion of the service quality. In this stage, the service encounter will confirm the previous telephone encounter when the guest evaluates the service quality. In this case the critical point will be the credibility and friendliness of the service employees in welcoming the guests. Then for the next service encounters (number 3- 5), the guest will experience the next interaction with the service employee when he or she is being escorted to the table and seated. In this case the body language matters most as there will be less verbal communication but more non-verbal communication. Researcher noted on the powerful influence of body language on giving impact on others. The impact someone makes on others depends on what he or she actually says (7%), how he or she says it (38%), and by his or her body language (55%). Besides, 93% of someone's emotion is communicated non-verbally without actual words. That is why it is of vital importance to pay attention to the body language and to make sure that the 'right' body language is shown during the service delivery. The body language can demonstrate whether the service employee is friendly, courteous and credible. As mentioned in the previous part it appears that some non-verbal cues are different from culture to culture. That is why it is imperative that the service employee is aware of multicultural cues and able to perform eventually the 'multicultural' body language depending on the situation. The 'right' body language will generate good service encounters. In the end, good service encounters accumulated over time maintain a long-term exchange relationship between customers and organization.

In the next service encounters (number 6-7), when the guest enjoys the meal, besides the tangible things like the meals served, decoration and atmosphere of the restaurant, the attentiveness and responsiveness of the service employees will be the important points the guest evaluates in judging the service encounter. The judgment of the service encounter will be positive when the guest's expectation is met or even exceeded.

In the last service encounters (number 8-9), even though it is the last 'moment of truth' but it is also a crucial moment to take care it will leave a 'good' or 'terrible' last impression about the overall restaurant service. When the service provider neglects this last crucial moment, it may happen that the last 'terrible' moment will distort the whole first 'good' impression.

CONCLUSION

Managing service quality has always been a target for most hospitality organizations in that it will result in customer satisfaction that very organization intends to accomplish. The more influence an organization has over its service quality, the better it will have control over its customer satisfaction. Service encounter or the 'moment of truth' is one of the predictors of service quality. It is a point in service delivery where there is an interaction between the service employee and the customer. Therefore, accomplishing a positive service encounter is very important. When the service provider is able to understand and meet customer's expectation, positive service encounter will be attained.

After analyzing the problems and challenges in managing service encounters, several points can be drawn in attaining positive service encounters:

1. Customers generally consider the way how the service employee or service provider performs recovery efforts, how adaptable the service employee or service provider is, how good is the spontaneity and how good the service employee or service provider is in coping customer's problems;
2. Adding more tangibility in the service encounter will minimize the risk of having a big gap between customer expectation and perception;

3. Non-verbal communication should be considered as 93% of the impression formed in the customer's mind is determined by non-verbal cues;
4. Cultural aspect is another point that will influence the service encounter. The ability for a service provider to respond culturally up to standard will be a strong point to develop a positive service encounter;
5. Purchase motivation is also another point to consider when attempting to manage service encounter as it contends with customer's expectation;
6. Last but not least, the effective use of service blueprint in managing the 'moment of truth' will help service provider trace some critical points in the 'moment of truth' when special attention is necessary so that the service provider will have more control over the service encounters. Even for more complicated hospitality organizations like hotels, for example, having detailed service blueprint for every service operation will help them have more control over service encounters and ensure service excellence.

CHAPTER 23

Personality Development Tips for Hospitality Professionals

EVERYONE IMPROVE HIS PERSONALITY

It is true that some people are gifted with charming personality. But it is also true that everyone can achieve an attractive personality. It is all about practice, determination and consistency. There are some easy ways to develop your personality -

Honesty

Firstly honestly think that you need or not need a developed personality. And then think about your strengths and weakness. Think about areas in which development is needed.

Determination

Determination is important factor in personality development. If you are determined you can definitely improve your personality. If your determination is weak you might lose your consistency.

Practice

Constant practice is the main key of personality development. If you get bore and leave practice you cannot improve. Personality development is not a work of one or two day. It is not a course of certain period. It is a life time process. So not get bore and keep practice.

"HERE ARE SOME PERSONALITY TIPS FOR YOU"

Confidence

Without self confidence your all efforts are useless for personality development. Your all good personality traits are useless. You are smart, intelligent and wise but don't look like this because of your lack of confidence, what is the use of your Smartness, intelligence and wisdom. Therefore improve your confidence first then do other practices.

Positive thinking

Always have a positive attitude in every condition. Most successful people are in the world are positive thinkers. With positive thinking you can eliminate all difficulties of your life but if you are a negative thinker there are many difficulties waiting for you. Choice is yours.

Good Qualities

God qualities always attract every one. So always try to achieve good qualities like honesty, politeness, time punctuality etc. if you always follow ethics or morals in your life you are ever recognized as good person even by bad persons.

Live a Healthy Life

Follow the rules of a healthy life style. Never forget unhealthy life style is a worst thing for a good personality. So follow healthy rules like

- Take always healthy meal.
- Take proper sleep.
- Do exercises daily.

Communicate Effectively

Communications skills are most demandable skills in today`s world. There are many ways to communicate with others like-

- Verbal
- Written
- Body language
- You should have good communications of all types if you want success in life.

TIME MANAGEMENT

Time management is an effective tool to enhance your life and career. Time is really a resource. You use it or not. Time is spending. If you use this resource effectively, we can help you in following areas related with time management.

- Decision making
- Education
- Meetings
- Health
- Job performance
- Project management
- Business success
- Knowledge
- Leadership
- Motivation
- Marketing
- Stress management

It simply means, how effectively we can use our time for best result in our business, job or in anything. If we can manage your time effectively, you can increase your business growth, you can complete your project in certain time and you can live a happier life. All successful people have good time management skills. There are two important things in time management.

- Writing effective resumes
- First impression
- Dress sense
- Communication skills
- Confidence building
- Soft skills
- Things to avoid in interviews

Set a goal and manage your time to achieve this goal

- Most people waste their time in unproductive activities like-
    - Watching television
    - Gossips
    - Unnecessary phone calls

You can enhance your career success with time management

Good time management is a crucial factor for career success. With the effective time management you can-

- Set your goals
- Know your priorities
- Organize your work
- Improve your work efficiency
- Complete the work in certain time limit

Here are some most common tips for effective time management

- Find out your time wasters.

- Without creating a goal you cannot be good time manager therefore always create a goal.
- Increase your determination to achieve a goal.
- Making to do list is a good idea for effective time management.
- Make a weakly review for keeping time managed.
- Make priority list
- Make urgent and important task list

TEAM WORK I

When a group of people performs an action to achieve same goal, this is called team work. Team work is very crucial for any developing or developed organization. Every effective team has a goal. Though every member has his personal goal but every personal goal leads to goal of the team.

Is pleasing personality important for professional life?

A group of people can create miracles for the organization, if every person works as a team member not as an individual. Take an example of a football team where every team member plays for a common goal of winning. It never win, if it loses characteristics, explained below:

- leader
- personal goal for every team member
- universal goal of win for a team
- cooperation
- clear plan and every player knows the plan
- limitations and priorities for every player

Characteristics of an effective team

- Communication Most important characteristic of a team is proper communication. If communication is clear and effective, certainly team work will be effective.
- **Cooperation feeling**: In an effective team, every member use others knowledge and he gives the benefit of his knowledge to others.
- **Leadership:** Every effective team has an effective team leader.
- **Positive atmosphere**: In a effective team, no space for gossiping. Every team member must have trust on others.
- **Goals**: Every effective team must have a clear goal. There can be many goals of team members to achieve this goal.
- **Motivation**: Team members of an effective team must be well motivated.

Why a Team Fails?

Only Working together of people is not team work. A team must have above defined characteristics. Sometimes we see that a team is unable to achieve its goals. Here we are discussing about the causes of failure of a team.

- Poor communication
- Lack of trust in team members
- Uncertain goals
- Ego problems
- Ineffective leadership
- Lack of new ides
- Member don't share their knowledge
- Difference in views

Characteristics of a Good Team Member?

- Encourages developing of other team member
- Take responsibilities for problems.
- Good communicator
- He has effective interpersonal skills
- Effective listener
- Knows his responsibilities, priorities
- He has respect for other team members and the team leader
- He has trust on others and never criticizes others.
- He have respect for opinions of other team member

TEAM WORK - II

When a group of people performs an action to achieve same goal, this is called team work. Team work is very crucial for any developing or developed organization. Every effective team has a goal. Though every member has his personal goal but every personal goal leads to goal of the team.

Team Work Skills

Every team member must have special teamwork skills. Here we are some most important teamwork skills for you-

Effective Communication

A team member must have communication skills. He must able to communicate his ideas, views, knowledge honestly and clearly. Here are some common tips:

- Make eye contact
- Respond to criticism politely
- Send clear massage

- Use appropriate volume
- Use simple language and words
- Respect your audience
- Be interested in people
- Criticize carefully and politely

Effective Listening

Like good communication, listening skills are also necessary for effective team work. Here are some tips for effective listening-

- Face the speaker
- Make proper eye contact
- Show interest in the subject and speaker
- Keep your mind focused
- Listen the main ideas
- Ask questions, if you don't understand the subject

Guidance, Support, Sharing

These are the most especial skills for any team member. A team member must be always ready for giving guidance and support for other team members. Every team member sharès his knowledge with other team members.

Commitment

Effective team members have commitment. He cares about the team and the goal of the team. He always be an active part of every activity of the team.

"How to be an effective team leader"

Every effective team must have an effective team leader. Team leader has a great impact on the working style and goals of the team. He represents the main idea of the team. Effective team leadership is not an easy task. He faces many challenges and problems in the leadership process. Effective team leadership quality needs particular skills. Here are some most important skills-

- Good communicator
- Have clear vision
- Interpersonal skills
- Motivational skills
- Integrity
- Decision making
- Goal oriented
- Confidence
- Empathy
- Problem solving.

Bibliography

Barnum, C and Wolniansky, N. (June, 1989), "Taking cues from body language", *Management Review*, 59-60.

Bebko, C. (2001), "Service encounter problems: Which service providers are more likely to be blamed?", *Journal of Services Marketing*, (15), 6, 480-495.

Brenner, R.C. (2001), "Body language in Business: How to sell using your body", *Brenner Information Group*, July 10, 2001

Grönroos, C. (2000), *Service management and marketing: A customer relationship management approach*, (2nd ed), Wiley, Chichester.

Hartline, M., Wooldridge, B. and Jones, K. (February, 2003), "Guest perceptions of hotel quality: determining which employee groups count most", *Cornell Hotel and Restaurant Administration Quarterly*, 43-52.

Hubbert, A. R., Sehorn, A. G. and Brown, S.W. (1995), "Service expectations: The consumer versus the provider", International *Journal of Service Industry Management*, (6), 1, 6-21.

Jafari, J. and Way, W. (December, 1994), "Multicultural strategies in tourism", *Cornell Hotel and Restaurant Administration Quarterly*, 72-79.

Kandampully, J. (2002), *Services management: The new paradigm in hospitality*, Hospitality Press, Pearson Education Australia.

Kotler, P., Bowen, J. and Makens, J. (2003), *Marketing for hospitality and tourism,* (3rd ed), Prentice-Hall, Upper Saddle River, NJ.

Lemmink, J. and Mattsson, J. (2002), "Employee behavior, feelings or warmth and customer perception in service encounters", *International Journal of Retail & Distribution Management,* (30), 1, 18-33.

Lovelock, C. and Wright, L. (2002), *Principles of service marketing and management,* (2nd ed), Prentice-Hall, Upper Saddle River, NJ.

Mattila, A.S. (1999), "The role of culture and purchase motivation in service encounter evaluations", *Journal of Services Marketing,* (13), 4/5, 376-389.

Price, L., Arnould, E. and Deibler, S. (1994), "Consumers' emotional responses to service encounters: the influence of the service provider", *International Journal of Service Industry Management,* (6), 3, 34-63.

Sundaram, D. and Webster, C. (2000), "The role of nonverbal communication in service encounters", *Journal of Services Marketing,* (14), 5, 378-391.

Tseng, M. M., Qinhai, M and Chuan-Jun S. (1999), "Mapping customers' service experience for operations improvement", *Business Process Management Journal,* (5), 1, 50-64.

Zeithaml, V. and Bitner, J. (2000), *Services marketing: Integrating customer focus across the firm,* (2nd ed), McGraw-Hill, Boston.

Zeithaml, V. and Bitner, J. (2003), *Services marketing: Integrating customer focus across the firm,* (3nd ed), McGraw-Hill, Boston.

Zeithaml, V., Berry, L. and Parasuraman, A. (1996), "The behavioral consequences of service quality", *Journal of Marketing,* (60), 31-46.